The Wisdom
of
Letting Go

The Path of the Wounded Soul

DEDICATION

This book is dedicated to Lesley Marsden. She is my niece, and my friend. Lesley is living so much of what this book is about, and she helped me by *the honest expression of her feelings.*

Kien Lam has also played a significant role in my learning to let go. He shares my pain. He is the brother I never had. And we've both learned that letting go *need not end a significant relationship.*

Finally, I dedicate this book to all my friends and colleagues who over the years have helped me work through the tough times–those dark nights that are then followed by even darker days.

Thank you all.

BUDDHIST PRAYER

Let all things be healthy
Let all things be peaceful,
Be sure to count your blessings at least once a day.

Forgive those who have hurt you,
And those who have offended you,

But forgive yourself for what you have done,
And let go of what you have failed to do.

That which is done there's no need to speak of,
That which is past there's no need to blame.

Have self-control, self-knowledge, self-respect,
The courage to dare,
Be tranquil, the light of intelligence will shine.

Strive to make the spot where you stand beautiful.
Then beauty and harmony will follow you
In all your ways and through all your days.

Buddhist prayer shared by Dang Jian-Wei,
Beijing, China

CONTENTS

INTRODUCTION

This book was inspired in the numerous workshops I conduct across the country:

> • *Fr. Leo, how do I let go of the man I was married to for twenty years?*

> • *When you know you are going to die, how do you let go of the fear?*

> • *I know I'm better on my own. But I still love her. Will I ever stop loving her? Will I ever be free?*

> • *Some days I want to let go of the anger. Other days I know I enjoy it. I'm confused. Is the anger me?*

How do we let go of the thousand and one situations that create the unhealthy baggage that weighs us down in life, stopping us from *living the moment*? This book seeks to be an answer.

In some chapters, I find myself expressing confusion, struggling in the gray areas of life, knowing the answer is not having a definite answer. Letting go does not mean we don't care. Letting go is discovering a path beyond the pain, beyond the conflict. *Letting go is finding a way to live life*.

I couldn't possibly have experienced all the situations I've written about, *yet I have feelings about them all*. So, as writers are supposed to do, I used my *imagination*. I imagined what it would be like to have AIDS, suffer an abusive husband, or feel the aching loneliness that comes with the death of a loved one. Life is interconnected, and I've lived long enough, suffered enough, hurt and been hurt enough, *to feel*. My imagination is rooted in my feelings.

The Wisdom of Letting Go is my ongoing journey, building upon my previous books that have discussed Spirituality and Recovery, Meditations for Compulsive People, and healing Religious Abuse. We all are searching for ways to move beyond the trauma, beyond the old messages, and beyond the limitations of obsessive behavior.

Many people have helped me write this book. They live in my memories and have played a significant role in my life–too, too many to mention. I've forgotten some of their names, but their faces and words are ever present. My numerous critics have also helped me grow. *We don't always like what we need!*

A special mention should be made of my editor, Cynthia Cavalcanti, for her critical eye and mindful sensibility; Jackie Hale, who devotedly typed the manuscript, and played a significant role in the book's design; and Anna Woo and Hilary Fitzsimmons, who struggled with my writing on a daily basis, and never complained. Thank you.

Wisdom is my goal. Already I'm thinking about writing a book of stories that emerge from the East. And you know *you're going to identify!*

Enjoy *The Wisdom of Letting Go*.

Leo Booth
October, 1999

Love

Chapter 1

Sometimes you must love somebody enough
to let them go.

I remember my mother saying this to me in the kitchen at my home in England. I was talking about a friend who for many years had been troubled with alcoholism, and how the fun that used to exist in our friendship had in recent years been transformed into anger, pain, embarrassment, and apathy. I had reached the point in every codependent's journey when I simply didn't care anymore. He was making me feel sick. As the Church hymn so aptly says, "We learn that love grows cold!"

I was telling my mother the friendship had given way to not caring; there was nothing more I could do for him, he had hurt me so much in recent years. I wanted out!

My mother said, "I know how you feel. That is how I used to feel about you!" She went on to share what it was like living with me, as a mother, when I was drinking. Then she stated powerfully: "This love requires *distance.*"

There is a point in "tragic love" when we need to pull back, separate the dysfunctional behavior from the individual we love, and create a powerful moment of distance. In this sense we "let go." And we do this not because we do not love, but *because we love*.

Nobody can change another person, or get another person to behave in the way we want them to behave. When those relationships become *really*—I mean *really*— painful, we must pull away and let go. Sometimes nothing positive happens, and the person simply gets worse.

But there are times, creative moments, when the separateness produces a miracle: we have given them the space to change—the donkey is drinking the water!

PRAYER

Great Spirit: You Who have given us the freedom to walk away from the pain that keeps on giving, may we see your creative power at work in the separateness.

*It's not that I don't love you; it's that I'm beginning
to love myself.*

Some of my earlier books deal with a cunning and powerful dysfunction I have called "religious abuse." Religious abuse keeps us separate from our true selves because it never allows us to really know who we are. I mean who we *really* are!

Religious abuse hurts and traumatizes us by overemphasizing sin, human failings, guilt, shame, and fear, but it does not tell us, in a manner we can hear, how we are loved with the power to love, how we are creative children of God with unlimited opportunities. Religious abuse tells us what we are not; spirituality tells us who we are!

Earlier I mentioned the word guilt. Often religion has emphasized how it is important to love others, even our enemies, but was less emphatic in stating we must also love ourselves.

Today, many of us are finding out we cannot really love another person until we have a healthy love and respect for ourselves. Indeed, sometimes we got the message we should stay married to, or involved with, people who were doing us serious physical and emotional damage. Many have died trying to love, for religious reasons, the abusive!

Only recently has popular therapy given us the clear insight that, more often than some of us care to think, we must let go of — or at least create a meaningful space between ourselves and — somebody we love. Not because we have ceased to love that person, but because we need to give some *quality attention* to ourselves.

If the other person could only see it, they, along with every other important relationship we have, would benefit when we first take time to develop a healthy love of ourselves.

In Zen logic: only when I love ME can I love You.

PRAYER

God, I am making the spiritual choice today to love myself. When I create this love energy within myself, I am truly connected to others.

For so many years, I would rant and rave about why God was not doing more to help the poor, needy, dying, and hungry; the prisoners of war; and victims of violence. And I always included a special plea for the helpless children of the world! If God is as powerful as we say He is, could it be that He has ceased to care? Could it be God is on the side of the abusers? Is God dead? How can God be God, yet allow the world to operate the way it does? Is there an answer to all the above?

Yes. Detachment.

God is not a codependent!

God is not a God who fixes, controls, intervenes, stops bad things from happening to good people, or makes everything safe.

Why? Because God knows that codependency — controlling love — does not work. Love requires freedom.

As human beings, God created us with the freedom, if we choose, to rob, steal, rape, and kill. Many people do some or all of the above. Connected to this idea of freedom is the possibility that any one of us could become the victim of aggressors, mad people, or those who feed and give energy only to their shadows.

And this is freedom. This is spiritual freedom.

Alongside this concept is the idea that human beings have been given the dignity to fight, if they choose, for those things that ennoble the hearts of the peacemakers, sweat and work for integrity and justice in all areas of life, and die for those ideals and dreams they believe are important. Greatness must be earned!

What kind of life would it be if God pulled every string to make us happy, protected us from all danger, and kept us safe from having to make decisions and take chances. That would be a life in hell. Think about it — no songs would be sung of the human adventure, no heroes or heroines would inspire future generations, the pain that feeds the soul of the poet would be quieted, and artists could paint only sunshine and joy. But what happened to the darkness and tears?

Freedom allows for the shadow. Detachment.

PRAYER

I embrace the power of Your detachment and make it my own. I know the spiritual journey involves letting go.

I'm willing to let go of my old relationships in order to have a spiritually passionate relationship with you.

We all carry baggage in our lives, and sometimes the baggage includes past relationships. Not all past relationships have been painful. They ended, or changed, for many reasons:

- *We simply outgrew one another.*
- *We journeyed in different directions.*
- *We found ourselves on different spiritual paths.*
- *We realized we need more than love.*
- *Death.*

All this being said, we sometimes need to be willing to let some, or all, of these past relationships go in order to discover the joy and freedom of a new and special relationship. Old baggage sometimes gets in the way.

When we say we are willing to let go of old relationships, we are not saying they were unimportant, harmful, or tainted in some way; rather, we bless those relationships and let them go to a place that is forever their own. What we are saying is that we are unwilling to force them, or awkwardly accommodate them, into a new relationship that is no less special, meaningful, or spiritual.

I've met many people who are able to bring together past relationships, past husbands and wives, lovers, and "first infatuations," and all mix and live alongside each other beautifully; but not everyone wants to do this, or is temperamentally able to achieve it.

If it starts to feel awkward to the point of irritability, then it's okay to let them (all of them!) go. Never jeopardize the passionate moment for a memory—no matter how much the memory titillates the ego.

PRAYER

Today I am unwilling to hurt those I love with personalities from my past. My intuition, spiritually illumined, tells me to let some people go.

I understand that to love you today does not include the acceptance of your past.

My inability to let go of the past was one of the main obstacles to my ability to change. How can you ever change when you cling to the past? Today I catch myself saying, often, as I look in the mirror, "Leo, you need to take out the old tape that is operating in your mind, and put in the new tape that will help you to change and face the future." We all come with a past, but we are not our past. *We are more.*

Today I am willing to accept my past, but that does not mean I must live in it. Acceptance is not a prison sentence! And, interestingly, although I believe it is important for me to accept *my* past, I'm not convinced it means I must accept *your* past. Please understand me, I'm not saying you cannot or should not be willing to accept the past behavior of another, but I'm not sure you are *required to* accept the past of another. Some things you cannot accept in another's past because you simply do not understand them. They are not things you can relate to. They are just confusing, or simply not okay with you. Period.

Healthy change means we moved from one state of existence to something more spiritual, and it feels better. A person can love me today but they do not, and I don't think I should expect them to, accept all and every part of my past.

The love that exists in the moment does not need to be anchored in the past. Thank God. When we are willing to move into a new reality, we are prepared to let go of that part of the past which never truly defined us. But we can only move on for ourselves; others must deal with their own pasts.

PRAYER

Spirit that dwells in the shadows and the light, today I know that no one thing from my past or future will ever fully define me. I am more than what I have done or will do. And it's okay.

In order for me to love myself, I need to be willing to forgive myself.

It took me a very long time to realize that for me to really love me—not respect or like me—but *really love me*, I needed to let go of some messages I'd heard in my childhood. I think the first unhelpful message was the idea that it is selfish to love yourself. The Church and family gave me the impression love was to flow *out of me* toward others. Only conceited people talked about loving themselves! For too many years I operated with this unhelpful mantra in my head.

Alongside the mantra was another dysfunctional message that went like this: "Your job is to forgive others, and God's job is to forgive you!" I never really heard, until quite recently, that the only forgiveness that really matters is *self*-forgiveness. Others can say they forgive you, and a Priest can mouth the statement, "God has forgiven all your sins," but if you don't *connect* with that forgiveness, then nothing really changes *feelings-wise*. You still *feel* the same—guilty!

Today I'm convinced I must let go of these unhelpful messages, and begin to understand we all make mistakes, and that I am not a mistake. We all do, say, and think things we later regret, but that is never who we are. Forgiveness comes when we understand this.

We are not alone in our failings. If I can forgive others, then I should use the same spiritual energy to forgive myself. "Lighten up, Leo. Don't be too hard on yourself. Get over the past and be willing to heal yourself for the future." Wow. The powerful statement Jesus used, "Physician, heal thyself," is now coming to life.

My willingness to entertain the idea that it is important for me to forgive myself came with a change in perception: *God's energy of forgiveness works through my choice to love myself in spite of the damaging things I have said or done.* With forgiveness comes the gift of freedom, and today I know love can only exist where freedom reigns.

PRAYER

God, I feel Your power operating through my mind, body, and emotions, and when I pronounce my forgiveness,

I experience Your shout for joy.

Love is like a box of chocolates; you never really know what you're going to get.

Love is complicated because it is so different for each person. I'm not suggesting there are not similarities in the way we love and the type of people we love, but no two loves are exactly the same.

I've heard many people say they experienced a great deal of pain in their lives because they tried to love in accordance with the thinking and ideas of others. Some people even married the person their parents "loved," or thought would be a good husband or wife. However, love is not only gentle and kind, it is also *personal*. Very personal. Other people cannot choose who you are to love.

The love that operates within me is a gift from God and it will be as different, unique, and individual, as I am different, unique, and individual. Love is not *sameness*.

This "Love Box" comes with many different flavors and in many different shapes: heterosexual, bisexual, homosexual, and yes, even nonsexual. These "forms" or "types" of love only touch the surface, because we all express love, and the need to have it expressed to us, in different ways. Is this making you feel confused? Do you feel it is all a mess and you wish God had created love to operate within clearly defined control systems? Do you wish God had not created the love energy at all? I hope not.

For me, the spiritual journey has involved accepting, and seeking to understand, these different and varied aspects of love, appreciating each subtle flavor. I'm so glad we have this variety. Also, I've discovered that at various stages in my life, I've felt these different and varied love energies — sometimes I'm quite shocked at what I like!

Would I really like all love experiences to look, feel, and act the same? Oh, God, no! Fear often lurks behind those who shout the loudest for conformity, and their fear is often rooted in a non-acceptance of themselves.

PRAYER

I celebrate and rejoice in the love child that emanates from within my need to play, making different music in my life.

You cannot force love.

When I first read this saying, I thought it was rather obvious. How can you force a person to love you? How can you force yourself to love somebody? But I didn't take loneliness into account.

When you are lonely, feeling separate and isolated, entering an empty house alone, not wanting to live after the death of your partner, not going out or taking vacations on your own, loneliness can kill life and substitute mere existence. Realizing for some people the love of another is what makes life livable, only then can you begin to understand why some people *force* themselves into love.

Today we call this behavior co-dependency. The person who forces himself or herself to love another, or puts pressure on another to love them, has not begun to acknowledge the Greatest Love: *when we begin to love ourselves.*

The above codependent behaviors do not really take into consideration the concept of self-love, where we naturally begin to experience the joy and pleasure of being with ourselves. Other people cannot make you really happy if you are not content with yourself.

For the person who knows the serenity that comes with finding the spiritual "at-one-ment" that comes with feeling relaxed and satisfied in our own skins, for this person, the word *force* could never be used in the same sentence as love. However, to reach this spiritual state, we must be willing to let go of many ideas most people have about love:

- *Love can only be found with another.*
- *Love involves family.*
- *To love yourself is unnatural.*
- *People who choose to live alone are selfish.*
- *The sole purpose of love is to produce children.*

When we let go of the pressure that forces us out of ourselves into the arms of others for the sake of love, will we be able to enjoy the thousand-and-one special moments that can only come with the genuine practice and experience of self-love: "Love God and your neighbor *as yourself.*"

PRAYER

Eternal Spirit, I found the peace that is beyond understanding when I found me.

Only then could I find You.

Love is not about perpetual agreement.

I grew up in the kind of home where disagreements were frowned upon, arguments avoided at all cost, and fighting was regarded as an abomination. Agreements were good. Spiritual. Close to the heart of God. Civilized.

The problem for me was that such an attitude was not only unrealistic, it was positively unhealthy. You can't live with other people, if you are to be *real* and not a fake, without having disagreements. I was soon to find out you could not love without having *some* disagreements, the occasional argument, and even the odd fight! When love involves passion, feathers will more than occasionally fly in all directions. Perpetual agreements only exist between people who do not *really* know each other!

However, because I was raised in this atmosphere of suffocating nicety, I was to walk away from significant love relationships because we disagreed, argued, or occasionally had a fight. And I found myself alone. Alone again.

When I look back on my love relationships, I am saddened by the fact that I really did not give those a chance to grow. I did not recognize the passion that created the disagreements, did not realize that love is not about — and never has been about — perpetual agreements. It is sad to now know I had love, but walked away because it was not always gentle, meek, or mild!

Today, thanks to a more universal understanding of spirituality and human culture, I'm aware love is about difference, diversity, energy in the heat of passion, and often strongly-held disagreements. Respect flourishes in the differences; rarely does respect grow in gentle sameness.

Today I love a good argument. I enjoy hearing opinions that are different from my own. I treasure the fact that most of the people I love are totally different in color and culture from me. I was looking for love in all the wrong places; I'm glad I discovered *passion*.

PRAYER

I embrace the energy of healthy disagreement, realizing the complexity of life, and the myriad options that make up what we call love.

Love requires humor if it is to grow.

If you ever doubted God has a sense of humor, take off all your clothes and look at yourself in the mirror. God, as perfect love, has a sense of humor. And really, if we are to love life, love people, and love the way nature develops and collides with human beings, it is essential for us to have a sense of humor. Otherwise, we would suffocate in our seriousness.

I think a sense of humor is involved in the concept "Let go and let God," because if we seek to control life, people, and the energy of nature, we will surely lose. And this letting go is the attitude needed to express love. Without a sense of humor, we will never be successful in love.

Today I refuse to treat myself too seriously. When I give lectures and seminars, I always look for opportunities to have fun with the audience, to make them laugh — often at my own expense. I am loving them through the humor. I jump on chairs, run from one end of the stage to the other, and dance with people who are expecting a serious lecture on spirituality. I've even worn the red nose of a clown.

I do similar things with the people I love in my personal life. I take them on mystery trips for lunch (they don't realize it, but often I'm lost myself); I kiss them on the nose while they are waiting in line for ice cream or movie tickets; I tell waiters the friend I'm having dinner with is really my father or mother; I play in life!

A college professor told me years ago that God created the world for fun, and when we can create fun in life and love, we are getting back to God's original intention for this planet. Most of the things that happen to us in life we have little control over, and most of the worries that kept us awake at night rarely came to pass.

Of course, I know there is a seriousness to life, and a seriousness to love, but I think we overemphasize the seriousness! When we let go of the control, love will grow.

PRAYER

God, I went to the toilet after my lecture with the microphone still switched on. A crowd of 500 shouted to me, "Flush the toilet, Leo."
We were connected in Your humor.

For years I thought being loved by others meant everything; today it is enough for me to love me.

I didn't realize how hard it is to grow up. Don't misunderstand me, I still enjoy the child in me playing and having fun, but I also need to grow up and take some responsibility for my life. It seems to have taken forever. Even now, in my fifty-third year at the time of writing, I'm not convinced I've got it right. Growing up is hard to do!

I was most childish in my effort to get people to love me. So much of my energy was spent working on people-pleasing, getting them to laugh, saying the right things, going miles out of my way to see that *they* arrived home safely, staying late at the most boring parties so I wouldn't disappoint the host, eating more cake than I ever needed in a month because the lady had "made it just for me."

On and on goes the saga of my trying to get people to love me by people-pleasing. It meant everything to me. Everything!

I carried with me, in my people-pleasing head, messages that make little sense today:

- *If people like you, you are a good person.*
- *Christians sacrifice their lives for others.*
- *Never disappoint people in their own homes.*
- *It's polite to laugh at jokes even if you don't think they are funny.*
- *Your life will be judged on how much joy and laughter you brought to others.*

Then somebody asked me, in a caring yet confrontational manner, "why is it so wrong for you to please yourself? When was the last time you did something for you—only for you—just because you deserve it?"

Of course I had to revisit my religion and confront my religious abuse in order to discover it was not wrong, sinful, evil, or selfish for Leo to love Leo. Today I find this is the center of my spiritual program: God does not make junk, and this includes Leo.

Now I spend my days doing good and wonderful things that enhance and sustain the quality of my life, and this self-love manifests itself in a dynamic love toward God and my neighbor.

PRAYER

God, I awake to give myself a big hug; now I am ready to go out and hug the world.

Love is more than a pizza pie.

I think I coined this awesome and provocative statement after listening to Dean Martin sing the song about knowing you're in love when you recognize the moon in your eye like a big pizza pie. They don't write songs like they used to!

But love is *more*. It is more than a pizza pie, more than friendship, more than money in the bank, more than being young and beautiful, more than righteous indignation, and more than racial purity. Love is God's energy — not merely energy, but *creative* energy.

Sometimes, in order to appreciate the power of love, we must be willing to let go of the unhealthy ideas long associated with the concept of love.

Today we affirm:

- *Love is not sex.*
- *Love is not about accepting less.*
- *Love is not always about being the most admired.*
- *Love often disappoints, and is occasionally confrontational.*
- *Love is not about being nice.*

The Wisdom of Letting Go

The power of love is discovered when we rise up and accept responsibility for who we are spiritually.

The power of love is knowing being positive and creative is a choice that needs to be made; it does not just happen.

The power of love is rooted in taking care of our minds, bodies, and emotions.

The power of love seeks to unite with God's energy in the ongoing creation of life.

The power of love seeks to confront all the "issues" of the world that disseminate hate and engender division.

The power of love affirms the gift of prosperity and the ability each of us has to manifest it.

The power of love is God's "Yes" to life, breathed into every creature on this planet and within the universe itself.

Prayer

Spirit of God, who at this moment I recognize as Love,
I accept You into my life and will express You in the
ongoing healing of the planet.

I realize the feelings of love I have for you are not enough.

It is really good for me to write about this topic because for so many years I thought love was everything, and if you were truly *in love,* everything would be okay. I sensed there was a lurking Pollyanna in me when I secretly cried in the movie *Love Story* at the words, "Love means never having to say you're sorry!"

Today I know love is not enough. Indeed, we can love more than one person, in many different ways. I also know I have loved, and in some cases still love, people who are not good for me. Indeed, they have caused me severe emotional pain. I realize love is not the same as infatuation, or "having a crush;" however, I still know love, in and of itself, is not enough.

Love, for me, needs to be accompanied by important spiritual words like respect, honesty, and communication, plus a deep respect for other people and this planet. Maybe some of you are already thinking when you use the word love, you automatically include those spiritual words, and in that case you might disagree with the opening sentence. However, the point I wish to emphasize is that you need not marry or "set up house" with a person just because you *love* them (here I'm using the word love in a restrictive romantic sense).

Because I am a romantic, I assumed that if you're engaged in a romantic relationship, it would inevitably proceed toward a "live in," and I experienced many years of pain as a result.

Today I am willing to let go of the rainbow definition: Love = live in, picket fence, apple pie cooking in the oven, and a log fire heating the thatched cottage. I want to include other qualities alongside *love* that make for a healthy and meaningful relationship.

Oh, yes, I still love (romantically) other people in my life, but I know such a love *alone* will never make me happy.

PRAYER

God, I embrace the concept of diversity in life and I'm happy knowing romantic love needs to be surrounded by other spiritual qualities to make a lasting relationship.

Love is a series of goodbyes.

At first this statement took me by surprise because I'd never really thought about love in the context of "goodbye;" rather, I associated it more with "hello!"

Upon deeper reflection, I'm understanding that as human beings we tend to use the word love in the context of people and situations:

• *I love Harry.*

• *I'm madly in love with the county of Hampshire, in England.*

• *I love the seasons.*

• *The love I have received from my family has continued to sustain me during the difficult periods of my life.*

Part of living the spiritual life is appreciating the various moments in our lives, and being grateful. Also, there is a sense that nothing lasts forever. We love our childhood, but there comes a time when we must grow up. We love our home and family, but there comes a time when we need to move out of the nest. We love the various boyfriends and girlfriends who make up the history of our love life, yet there comes a time when we must move on; even the marriage that lasted fifty years will come to an end as we then embark on our continued journey through the door of death. When we think about it, love really is a series of goodbyes.

As I was writing this reflection, I was acutely aware some people might find this thought terribly depressing, but I think it is an important part of life that needs to be faced. At the heart of love is the aspect of letting go. If we cling to the past, or hold on like grim death to the present, we can never fully appreciate the ongoing adventure of the spiritual journey.

Of course, a person could protest that we still have our memories, and that is undoubtedly true. But we really have moved on. From our childhood home, the friends we played with at school, the first kiss, the children we were gifted with and have let go to create their own lives, the marriage that brought so much happiness and joy, even the pain and sadness in life. Sure we still have our memories! True. What would life be like without our memories? But that is exactly what they are—*memories*. A memory is a spiritual connection we have moved beyond, signifying the moment of goodbye.

Our goodbyes in love need not be sad or depressing; rather, we should thank God for the times we had, and the myriad opportunities that await us, even after death.

PRAYER

As I am grateful for the many hellos I make in my life, so I am grateful for those important goodbyes that have produced fond memories.

Love is letting go of unrealistic expectations.

Like so many people, I like to think I am an incurable romantic, and I know fantasy plays a healthy and important part in my life. I dream my dreams, and some of them are truly wonderful, but not a few are unrealistic. And this is okay. Please understand I am not being restrictive when I write this, because I also know we should not place limitations on who we are, what we can achieve, and the life we can create. Indeed some of my fantasies, even the unrealistic ones, have a purpose, and they give me great pleasure:

• *Imagining I have the popularity of Charlie Chaplin, or will achieve the social and spiritual impact of Mother Teresa or Albert Schweitzer.*

• *Believing I have the body and energy of Leo twenty years ago.*

• *Believing my health is not related to what I smoke, eat, or drink.*

Fantasy is not necessarily an unhealthy ingredient in life, but it can soon develop into unrealistic expectations that disappoint and cause pain. I suppose the spiritual word that needs to be embraced at this point is *balance.*

In context, this means knowing when our love fantasies have moved into the unhealthy arena that can so easily create diminishment. These are the dreams, hopes, and fantasies I believe we should be willing to let go.

In my book entitled *Spirituality and Recovery*, I remember saying spirituality is reality, and I still believe this to be true. Anything, especially a love relationship, that is unrealistic for everyone concerned is going, eventually, to bring damage and pain:

• *Expecting to have a meaningful and healthy relationship with an active alcoholic or drug addict is an unrealistic expectation.*

• *Expecting a relationship to grow without spiritual values and boundaries is an unrealistic expectation.*

• *Wanting your children to love and respect you because you shower them with money, gifts, and a stream of codependent excuses for their selfish behavior is an unrealistic expectation.*

• *Affirming a prosperity consciousness that does not include co-creative responsibility, work, and tough choices is an unrealistic expectation.*

How do you know when an expectation is unrealistic? This is the spiritual question. It involves a knowing of yourself, the nurturing of intuition, and the strength to see people and situations clearly and *in context*. Thinking you are somebody other than your true self is a recipe for disaster. Thinking others are different from their true selves is equally dangerous.

PRAYER

Today I let go of all unrealistic expectations in order to discover the fantasy at the heart of all true reality.

Love makes the world go around when you realize you're not the only one pushing.

I've always felt a sense of quiet satisfaction when I've heard the above expression. It suggests love is the powerful emotion that not only makes for joy and meaning in the world, but actually makes the world circulate, actually makes the world go round, and round, and round!

As I write this, I have a visual image of a miniature Planet Earth, spinning in the sky, with "love heart" shapes encircling it. The reality is that love, respect, integrity, and spirituality are the ingredients that heal a divided world, and it is this expanded sense of the word "love" that makes life worth living.

The concept that will always destroy and separate our world is the idea that only one understanding of love is right, only one religion can deliver the God of love, there is only one way to make relationship, only one proper way to sexually express ourselves, or only one way to live life and experience the universe.

Another point that needs to be considered is that we need not love in isolation. The value of the love experience is in the way it connects people to one another. We need to let go of the idea that we can go it alone. Whether we are talking about the love of a person, family, or the planet, it makes much more sense if we can bring together our friends and colleagues in the love expression.

I don't know about you, but I feel really satisfied when I can share the people I love with my friends and "fellow travelers." I'm not happy keeping people in rigid and separate compartments. This is also true for ideas. I truly love the concept of spirituality, and when I am able to share my ideas with other people, I am truly enriched.

In recent years, because I am often in the company of Buddhists, Hindus, or people from a Native American culture, I have been able to develop and connect with a more comprehensive understanding of God, a rich tapestry of what Divinity can mean. This willing acceptance of diversity, especially as it relates to the manifold experiences of love in the world, has become a most treasured gift.

PRAYER

Today I am learning the art of not simply hugging other people, but linking my ideas with others in the divine experience of love.

Some people say love is not about sacrificing yourself for another. However, there has always been a 'great love' that involves sacrifice.

In recent years all of us have been helped by the many articles and books that have been written on the dangers of codependency: having a love experience that is *always* aimed in the direction of others, and does not "take care" of who we are. A love without healthy boundaries, we are told, is ultimately destructive!

And this is true. However, the concept of balance encourages us to realize there also exists a kind of love that is so divinely pure, that it willingly will sacrifice itself for others. It is rare. And there is always a discussion that can ensue concerning what is deemed "divinely pure." Many unhealthy sacrifices have been demanded from people in the name of God, or some all-consuming religious dogma.

Yet we see in the person Jesus, and in other religious and political figures, some values that are so important they override personal safety, family, community, and even life itself. The poets have often regarded this as the ultimate expression of love: "God so loved the world that He gave His only begotten son that we might not perish."

During the Nazi years, and times in which Communist expansion was affecting the lives of so many populations, there were some men and women who were willing to give their lives for spiritual values they felt were more important than family or life itself. I'm sure, had they first had a discussion with friends or even religious leaders, these "saints" would have heard:

• *But you are only one person and…*

• *What will become of your wife, husband, children…*

• *Is there not another way of keeping your integrity without sacrificing your life?*

Heroes, saints, martyrs — where would the world be without those men and women who turned their faces away from personal safety and were willing to make the ultimate sacrifice? They were willing, and in some cases joyously willing, to *let go* of everything. Here we are confronted with a love that is beyond *normal* comprehension, yet we recognize it as being noble, nay, even divine!

PRAYER

I hope I would be willing, when confronted with an evil, or situation that required the ultimate sacrifice, to find the courage to let go of this life.

I seek a responsible love, not a controlling infatuation.

I like to think I am growing up, and part of growing up for me is being responsible, i.e., having the ability to respond! For too many years I wanted things to go my way, in my time, according to my words and my ideas, and others were great if they agreed with me. My insistence that things go my way extended to people. If I liked them, I expected them to like me; if I loved them, I expected them to love me. Everything was on *my* terms.

It's sometimes hard to face up to the fact that I had a controlling infatuation that really robbed people of their freedom and dignity. Love was far more about receiving than it was about giving!

This is slowly changing. We have all loved and lost. We've all gone through the experience of losing something special because our ego or control got in the way and suffocated an aspect of life that now, with the benefit of hindsight, we miss terribly. Oh, if only we could revisit the past and respond differently, act differently, and choose different words. If only...

However, rarely can we go back, so the spiritual response to these painful experiences is, "did we learn from them?" If we keep doing, acting, and saying the same things, we will keep getting the same results. Change is an important part of living the responsible life.

Today I'm willing to let go of my controlling infatuations, the many times when my heart was not guided by my head, those times "I want" or "I must have" rarely included the needs of others. I am willing to let go of those moments, yet learn from them.

Letting go does not mean we do not remember, or are unwilling to learn from the past; rather it does mean we choose not to live in the pain of the dysfunction. We've all experienced the all-consuming, controlling infatuations, just as we've all had temper tantrums and vindictive thoughts—but that is not who we are.

A responsible love is based on respect, freedom, space, and personal dignity that I am willing to afford others.

PRAYER

Oh God, your healing power that exists within me allows me to rise above those behaviors that hurt and cause pain.

Love will always surprise; it is a mystery.

We've probably all heard the song "Love is a many splendored thing." I suppose the song became immensely popular because it resonated with so many people. It certainly resonates with me. I don't think I could live in a world without the love of family, friends, a lover, God, or the poets.

Really, when we sit and think about it, love is the most powerful energy in the world, and it is something we can all relate to at one time or another. Love is life!

Yet, I often ask myself, "what is it?" Once I think I have a definition, something else pops up and I'm forced to begin the process of redefining, and so the saga has gone on throughout my life.

Love is not always happy; often it is painful. Love is not sensible; often it is crazy. Love is not always clear; often it is confusing! Love is a mystery.

Also, you never quite know when it will reveal itself, where it will come from, or what it will look like. It's not that love is a surprise — love *is* surprise!

I've decided to let go of trying to understand love, or seek a clear and precise definition; instead, I'm happy just experiencing it.

A friend who had been divorced for twenty years, and really didn't expect to have a romantic love in her life again, recently went to South Africa for a vacation.

There she met a young man, working at the bank where she was changing her travelers' checks. That "certain feeling" hit her. He was fifteen years her junior.

They had dinner. Fell in love. Married within six weeks. And to this day they are supremely happy. Who would have thought it!

So you, the reader, who may be feeling love has passed you by, that no new love interest will come along, do not give up. Love *is* surprise!

PRAYER

God, you have given us so many surprises in life, not least the precious gift of love. Today I express my gratitude.

God is love. God is detached. Love involves detachment.

I remember hearing from my professor in England that God is detached, and I did not really understand what he meant. But today I think I understand.

When I look at the depth of pain and suffering so many people experience — the wars and killings that affect not only soldiers but their loved ones; the natural disasters that destroy towns, villages, countries, and entire islands — the only way I can make sense of this world is to believe God *loves with detachment.*

I've been informed about this concept by the many books and articles written on codependency. God is not a codependent. God is not using divine energy to fix, control, hinder, or "take away magically" our pain. This is not to say God does not love us; rather, God loves us enough to *let us go.* God allows us the freedom to confront our inhumanity toward each other. God created the responsible men and women who have risen up to lead us to another spiritual level — Mother Teresa, Mahatma Gandhi, and Martin Luther King, for example.

God creates the space for us to figure out ways to get along.

I believe in this spiritual detachment, though I know I don't always want it. In fact, I often hate the freedom God has granted us, yet, on my better days, I know it is spiritual. Detachment allows for a personal and communal dignity that fosters growth and responsibility.

This is the perfect love. It is not controlling, manipulative, or suffocating; rather, is it the essence of freedom. I'm not, and neither are you, a puppet on a string. God does not make us happy, prosperous, talented, or loving. That is our responsibility.

PRAYER

I accept the gift of Your detachment and I seek to reflect the same in my life. My detachment is often a confusing aspect of my genuine love and caring.

Codependency

Chapter 2

I am seeking the spaces within our togetherness.

Kahlil Gibran suggested in order to have a healthy and creative relationship, it is important to discover those places that are *ours,* separately — those quiet places to which we can return for our own growth and sustenance.

When I first heard people talking about codependency, I did not think it was an important problem. Certainly it did not seem to rank alongside alcoholism, drugs, or sexual abuse. In recent years, I have changed my mind, because it seems to me if we are not able to find that quiet place within ourselves, we will forever be in search of that certain something outside ourselves, and this leads to the myriad addictions with which we are all too familiar.

When it comes to the issue of relationships, the problems that develop from a clinging and suffocating attachment are all too numerous, often leading to the death of the relationship. Gibran put his finger on the solution, as did Jesus when he suggested we love God and our neighbor alongside a healthy love of ourselves. When we take time out to love ourselves—listening to the music we *enjoy*, having a meaningful *walk* on the beach, taking time to go on a retreat for *our own* spiritual needs, continuing to enjoy friends we have *outside* the relationship—when we take time out to explore our own space, we are able to return to the relationship with more energy and joy.

I suppose the engine that drives codependency is fear. Somewhere in our minds, we have the idea if we are not physically *with* another person, either the love will die or the person will seek comfort in another. *Fear will eventually create its own reality.* The truth is something very different, because when we create our own space, when we allow the loved one to explore who they are, we both become the winners.

As I write this, I'm obviously thinking of a lover; however, it is true for all our relationships. When we create that important spiritual space for friends and colleagues to explore their lives, we all become the richer.

Knowing this is the beginning of wisdom.

PRAYER

God, You who have created the spaces in our lives, know that I am truly grateful. Following Your divine example, I seek to create the important spaces for those I love.

I am realizing I am <u>not</u> responsible for how you feel.

This was a very hard lesson for me to learn. All my life I had grown up believing I was responsible for your happiness, joy, sorrow, excitement, and tears. The list went on and on. I never really understood that *you* have a choice in life, and that *you* are responsible for your feelings.

Feelings were never really discussed in my home, church, or university. Even when I went to theological college, and we had long lectures on spirituality, faith, and relationships, the topic of feelings rarely, if ever, came up. I was ignorant of my feelings, and yours. I certainly did not know who was responsible for the feelings that always manifested themselves. It was easier simply to blame myself!

The above statement tells me clearly that I am responsible for how I live, what I say, and the actions I take. This includes my feelings. But I am not responsible for the feelings *you* have. It is somewhat arrogant to assume I am responsible for your feelings, because they are yours!

Of course, the statement is not saying my actions, behavior, and speech do not affect you. One cannot live alongside another, or in community, without being affected or influenced by others—but *your response* to life and people is yours. Your responsibility.

The force of this statement prompts people to examine where they are in their lives, and whether they are living and operating in a "safe place." Choice is a powerful spiritual word, and it is so intimately associated with responsibility. If we feel sad, happy, angry, joyous, guilty, etc., then we need to take responsibility for healing and nurturing these feelings.

It is no longer acceptable to blame others for your twenty years of unhappiness because spiritually we will be asked *why* we allowed ourselves to stay in those situations for so long. Equally, we will be encouraged to take pride in the joy and happiness we have created by staying in certain relationships with healthy friends and colleagues.

Truly we are learning the wisdom of the statement: "We teach people how to treat us." This includes and affects our feelings.

PRAYER

Spirit God, who created me with feelings that need to be expressed in a healthy environment, today I accept and take responsibility for them.

Control is really about neediness.

After reading *Women Who Love Too Much*, I thought codependency was about passive people who couldn't say "no," and gave love but couldn't get their own needs met. People who loved too much were weak! *Passive* people can be controlling in their apparent "weakness," and very manipulative. In addition, there is a form of codependency that often is not talked about that is *overtly controlling*, often violent, yet equally needy.

Control is the opposite of freedom. When one person seeks to control another, passively or overtly, that individual is revealing insecurity. Love, affection, or friendship should never be based on the need to control, manipulate, or take away choice from another person. This is not only true in marriage, or significant relationships, but also in church and government.

In *When God Becomes a Drug*, I discussed how some clergy, because they are insecure or needy, control their congregations with Bible laws or church dogma that sometimes do not bear scrutiny. Manipulating a person's belief in God is a most deceptive form of codependency.

I've also seen many men (and women) use violence or abusive language to keep their partner in fear, to assert domestic control. Yet they are really revealing their neediness:

• You will never leave this house. Who would want you?

• Your stupidity forces me to punish you. You are so stupid. Have you thought where you would be without me?

• Can't you do anything right? What would happen to you if I were not here to correct you?

• I know you are angry and feeling sad now. But one day you will thank me for this beating.

These are all tragic statements that reveal a *needy* human being. Thanks to therapy in the last twenty years, and understanding the unhealthy messages we take into adulthood from our dysfunctional families of origin, many of us are learning to let go of the control. If we offer the gift of freedom, and a person chooses to stay, we know they are there because they want to be.

Codependent neediness is rooted in insecurity and fear. Knowing this is the beginning of the healing process. Individuals are learning how to relate to each other differently; more church ministers share authority with their congregations; parents are seeking to talk and express their feelings with their children; so many past insecurities are being replaced by healthy boundaries and respect.

PRAYER

I know I need love but I am not needy; my past neediness is being replaced by a respect for freedom.

For too many years I have placed others at
the center of my life.

Why did I do it? Why was it so important for me to make you happy, stop your tears, and not do anything to disappoint you? Why?

Because my self-esteem was at an all-time low. I could blame my religious abuse with its emphasis upon sin. I could blame my people-pleasing family of origin. I could certainly blame my alcoholism and the guilt and shame it induced in my life. It was probably a combination of all these things, and many others as well. All I know is that when I heard somebody talk about codependency, light bulbs went on in my brain: *I had it!*

Hearing about codependency really helped me to talk about my neediness, especially in the group work I have been involved with over the years. Talking about my codependency and neediness made it come to life, and I was able, with the help of others, to see it all too plainly. I was able to revisit my past behavior.

It wasn't too long before I realized I did not love Leo, did not really respect Leo, did not really know Leo. Wow.

This was scary, and it was also true.

Then somebody said to me, "Why don't you throw away the old tapes, and write healthy tapes to play in your mind. *You* must create the healthy tapes that make sense to you."

• *So I started with affirmations.*

• *And I wrote poetry.*

• *Then I created positive prayers I could use in the morning, and at night before I went to sleep.*

• *Before long I began to associate with people who had self-esteem and a healthy ego.*

• *Eventually I was giving Leo a big kiss in the mirror before I left for work every morning.*

Leo was at the center of Leo's life.

It's funny (tragically) how many people spend their whole lives trying to meet the needs of others, and rarely do much for themselves. It's as if they are not important. As somebody once said: "When the codependent goes home alone, nobody is there!"

Yet when you find your center, and your center is you, you enjoy life so much more. You laugh more, create more, earn more, travel more, see more — the center is the place of *more*.

PRAYER

God, I share with You my love of life, and it began when I discovered the beauty and power that exist within me

Let go – and get a life.

I'm sure we've all encountered the saying "Let go and let God." While I enjoy this provocative statement, I think it requires a certain amount of explanation.

"Let go" does not mean we have no responsibility. We mustn't expect God to pay the rent, find an attractive lover for us, make the university examination questions easy, or keep us healthy.

"Let go and let God" is really a co-creative statement in the sense that when we let God into our lives we are more than willing to stand up to the plate!

It is in this sense I also mean, "Let go – and get a life." The act of letting go can be a very positive response to all those challenges that confront us, especially in our relationships, because it signifies we are prepared to do something:

• *We are willing to let go of all the excuses we have made for our lazy and irresponsible children.*

• *We no longer will remain in a relationship where we are not respected or treated with dignity.*

• *We let go of a God who is only judgmental and angry.*

• *We let go of blaming others for unhealthy choices we have continued to make.*

• *We are willing to let go of an unhealthy use of food or alcohol.*

In this sense, letting go becomes a positive and creative action that produces spiritual results in our lives. It does not mean putting our hands in the air and appearing helpless.

The Serenity Prayer says it beautifully: we accept the things we cannot change, and find the courage to the change the things we can. We let go of the rigid control that has us playing God, in order to be free to live life in all its fullness.

When we stop meddling in other people's stuff, and actively involve ourselves in living *our* lives, then great expectations are made real.

PRAYER
When I let go in my life, I take on the
spiritual responsibility to live my life with
dignity and passion.

*I'm wondering why I say "Yes," when I really
mean "No." Today I'm willing to confront
this behavior in order to become real.*

Of course I'm understanding the reason I say "Yes" to
so many people when I should really respond with
"No," (in some cases a most emphatic "No"), is that I
want to be liked. I don't want to disappoint. God, I'm
over fifty years of age and I'm still a people-pleaser!
Why? Well, I think I received the message early in life
that if you wanted to succeed, you have to please people.
My parents were people-pleasers, my sister still is a
people-pleaser, and my church background encouraged
me with the idea that *sacrifice*, regardless of why or how,
is good.

But this doesn't fully address the people-pleasing
mentality. There is the issue of self-esteem, or, more
importantly, the lack of it. I grew up with the feeling of
not being good enough, with a discomfort about who I
was. This led to my abuse of alcohol and the destructive
codependent behavior I've struggled with for years. *And
being a priest did not help.* I kept confusing self-love with
selfishness. God forbid people should think I was a
selfish priest!

Today I'm understanding it is okay to say "No" to some people and, more importantly, to say "Yes" to my life. How can I ever be available to others if I'm not available to myself?

A friend once asked me to tell lies to his wife in order to protect an adulterous relationship in which he was involved. I felt really awkward. My initial response, because he'd been a friend for many years, was to oblige. But the more I thought about it, the more I saw how I was being abused.

The following day I called him and said, "No." I would not tell lies. I also did not approve of the double life he was living.

This was a most important step in my letting go of people-pleasing behaviors, and old tapes that still operate in my head. The wonderful thing happening as I seek spiritual growth and personal honesty is that most of the people to whom I say "No" — people I confront — seem to respect me.

The friend who was cheating on his wife recently called to say he admired my response, and has recently gone into counseling with his wife, confessing his past extra-marital relationship. Maybe the old-timers were right when they said honesty is the best policy. This includes honestly expressing our feelings.

PRAYER

Lord, I know I want people to respect me, but it is more important, today, for me to respect myself.

*Unhealthy religion has played a significant role
in keeping me sick.*

This may seem a strange thing to say, especially for a priest, but I remind you to notice the key word "unhealthy." I'm not talking about a healthy religion that allows for discussion, disagreements, inclusiveness, and tolerance. I'm talking about a dysfunctional system not a few of us associate with our families of origin. The child who grew up in a dysfunctional home heard:

- *Don't talk.*
- *Don't trust.*
- *Don't feel.*

In a similar way, the dysfunctional church creates the following:

- *Don't think.*
- *Don't doubt.*
- *Don't question.*

It's painful to think how many people developed their insecurities in the family, but it's even more scary if our insecurities are rooted in what we were told about God, discipleship, and sin.

The Wisdom of Letting Go

We hear so much today about guilt and shame, and how they affect our behavior and attitudes, especially with regard to codependency; but can we really expect to understand guilt, shame, and codependency without exploring religious abuse?

For many this is a new subject. People have come to me after I've given a lecture on unhealthy religious practices saying: "I've never heard anybody talk about religious addiction and religious abuse. Wow!" Yet the same people often refer to themselves as *recovering* Catholics, *recovering* Baptists, or *recovering* Jews!

If we are willing to begin the healing from religious addiction and religious abuse, we must be willing to let go of the old religious tapes that overemphasized sin at the expense of spiritual power and glory. It is not enough to say we suffered religious abuse; that will only keep us victims. We must reconnect with a loving God, and reflect that God in our prayers and conversations.

PRAYER

God of the Universe, religion is an instrument that can wound or re-connect us with our specialness and divinity. Today I seek to reflect a healthy relationship with You.

God is not a codependent.

Codependency is an unhealthy relationship that is the opposite of love and personal integrity. Rather than experiencing our personal power and innate specialness, it seeks to control and disempower, often for selfish or insecure reasons.

This is not the kind of relationship God wants with any of His (Her) children.

• *Because God is powerful, God wants us to be powerful.*

• *Because God is creative, God wants us to be creative.*

• *Because God is lovingly detached, God wants us to be lovingly detached.*

• *Because God freely forgives, God wants us to freely forgive.*

God is not a codependent. Nor is God the overprotective lover who rushes in to fix our every problem or confusion. God knows the spiritual journey will involve pain and feelings of isolation.

God gives us the freedom to make mistakes that affect not only our lives but the lives of others.

God knowingly allows bad things to happen to good people.

God gives us the space to make choices that can destroy our health and the well-being of others.

God is not a codependent.

Some people pray for a God to be more controlling, involved, and manifest in the things that are good and healthy in their lives. I believe these prayers to be, in the long term, spiritually disastrous.

Much better *for us to struggle* with what is good or evil, actions that enable or destroy, thinking that is positive or negative, or the shadow and light of our own personality. Only in this way can we co-create, in relationship with God, *the good life*, producing men and women who are seen to be saints, in every generation.

PRAYER

God, sometimes I want You to come and fix my life,
remove my problems, and make my path
straight and clear. But in my better moments,
I know it is in the challenge and effort of life
that my glory and power are made manifest.

To love myself, especially to say it out loud, is not a sin.

Why must we make a distinction between having a healthy love of others and loving ourselves?

An aspect of religious abuse, or spiritual abuse, is the message we heard long ago that if we spend time *simply on ourselves*, that is sinful. If we spend money on ourselves, taking vacations or buying expensive clothes, that is extravagant.

The abuse tape seemed to suggest love is only in relation to others, and should not be aimed at ourselves.

I heard people on a recent recovery cruise say out loud:

• *If I spent time or money on myself, I felt guilty.*

• *As a wife and mother, I was expected to be there for others, but not there for myself.*

• *For years I felt so stressed because I did not know how to ask for my "quiet time."*

• *Work in my home was seen as a virtue; relaxation and rest was viewed as laziness.*

• *My job as a father was to "take care of" the house, wife, children, and finances. Nothing in my childhood told me to take care of my own needs.*

• *My mother told me before I got married that, as a wife, I was expected to satisfy the needs of my husband. Only in the last five years have I heard the message that I have sexual needs; I need to be loved.*

I can relate to all the above statements in one way or another. It seems to me that a national healing has begun. More and more people are saying in support groups, and on spiritual retreats, that it is okay, indeed, it is essential, for them to begin the process of loving themselves.

And they are saying it out loud!

I've heard some people say it is sad that we need to support each other or use affirmations for the self-obvious need we all have, i.e., to love ourselves. Never mind. Thank God it is happening now, so future generations get the message.

PRAYER

God, today I love myself… and I love myself out loud.

Real love should not hurt so much.

Often I am asked, "Why does love cause me so much pain? So much distress?" We all know you cannot love another without having times of pain and sadness; however, the distress should not *define the relationship*!

When we address any dysfunction in a Twelve-Step program, we use as our measuring stick two words taken from the first step: powerless and unmanageable. We know we have a drinking problem when we experience, *on a consistent basis*, feelings of powerlessness and unmanageability. We know we have an eating disorder when we experience, *on a consistent basis*, powerlessness and unmanageability around food. The same with sex, gambling, and shopping! This also applies to codependency. When we are involved in a codependent relationship, we experience, on a consistent basis, feelings of unmanageability and powerlessness — the relationship simply hurts *too much*!

We've already discovered *love is not enough*. This is particularly true if the love is unhealthy. A love without boundaries — needy, controlling, abusive, followed by

The Wisdom of Letting Go

apologies — will only get worse, and could be fatal.

As with all addictions, it is possible for healing to begin, but there must be a change in behavior for both parties, because if we keep doing the same things, we will only get the same results. Often a physical space is required to change behavior, and establish new thinking patterns to establish a healthier togetherness. I recommend attendance at Al-anon or codependency meetings. Sometimes a gentle therapist, who can explore family history and possible dysfunction, will also be necessary.

These measures begin the process of healing a painful relationship . And yes, there are times when there is an unwillingness in one or both parties, in which case the healing will require *permanent* separateness. Sometimes we must love enough to let them go!

Spirituality is about being a positive and creative person, building positive and creative relationships, and we cannot experience this if we are consistently in pain. We are responsible for bringing health into our relationships, and sometimes we will never experience the joy and serenity we long for in life, without letting go. As the song says, we were never promised a rose garden!

PRAYER

Great Spirit, as You energize creation, You show me, often through pain, the choices and changes I must make in order to be free.

I'm an educated person, yet I've never had a lesson on boundaries.

I suppose you cannot ever really understand codependency without knowing something about boundaries, even if what you learn is that you don't have any! In some ways this is not surprising, because so few of us ever had lessons on boundaries, what they are, and why they are important.

As a priest in training, I can remember going to many lectures and workshops in England, yet I don't remember ever hearing anything about boundaries. The word was only used in the context of nations and geography!

It doesn't take a genius to realize because we live *in relationship*, the respect we give each other, and the space we create to make a person feel safe, is essential. Also, feelings can be invaded by the more subtle aspects of abuse — silence, shouting, sarcasm, and passive-aggressive comments. Without boundaries, nobody can be really healthy, and a relationship between God, self, and others demands healthy boundaries.

Because I was a late learner, I know I'm not too good at creating healthy and respectful boundaries. However, the following guidelines have proven most helpful:

• *Don't interrupt a person when they are speaking.*

• *Ask permission (unless you know the person very well) before you give a hug.*

• *Never use racist or sexist language, even if you mean to be funny.*

• *Allow for space in your relationship, and speak up if you feel your space is being invaded.*

• *Don't expect people to guess at what you are feeling or thinking – speak up.*

• *Avoid gossip.*

• *Listen attentively to what people are saying to you, and tell them if you are too busy to be really present.*

• *Don't stuff your resentments. Speak your truth as you see it and feel it.*

Because I was not educated during my younger years about the significance of boundaries, I have needed a great deal of help in my later life. It's not always been easy for me to ask for help, but a friend shared, "Leo, it's in your own interest, and in the interest of others!" He is so right.

PRAYER

God, the healthy boundaries You have created with us, I seek to emulate in my life.

Where does my life end and my family begin?

I can remember pondering this thought when I was drinking. I'm convinced that codependency, the inability to create healthy relationships, the constant giving away of our spiritual power, is fed and sustained by unhealthy actions and behaviors.

Alcoholism, because it revolves around guilt, shame, arrogance, anger, and fear, feeds the unhealthy codependent spirit and destroys all boundaries.

Neediness is followed by the people-pleasing, withdrawal, guilt, and anger that lead back to neediness, and the sick cycle begins again. All of this makes it so difficult to know where self-hatred begins and enmeshment follows. In most cases, the family is equally sick, so they are dancing with the disease to similar music!

• Let go of the behavior that is creating unmanageability and powerlessness, and embrace the 'tough love' principle of personal responsibility.

- *We need to trust our instincts, once we have moved away from the alcohol or similar dysfunction, and develop behavior that clearly benefits our lives.*

- *Follow a spiritual plan that matches behavior with affirmations, and behavior with a positive attitude.*

- *Perhaps with therapy, we will understand we belong to a family, but we are not the family; we do not have sole responsibility for the health and happiness of that family.*

- *Always we should surround ourselves with healthy friends who will lovingly point out when codependent enmeshment is raising its ugly head.*

- *At an appropriate time, only if it feels safe, we should be able to sit down and explain to our families why we have changed our attitudes and behaviors, explaining we do this not to seek permission, but clarification.*

I'm convinced what we perceive as an unhealthy and stressful situation concerning our family will also be operative among those we love, our employment colleagues, and our friends. Therefore, the action of letting go of dysfunctional behaviors and developing a positive lifestyle will become a life process.

PRAYER

Divine Spirit, I acknowledge the work I have achieved in my ongoing recovery from codependency, realizing on a daily basis the gift of healing involves my cooperation.

Spirituality sometimes requires us to disappoint.

I tell you the truth, sometimes the hardest thing I had to do was disappoint another person by saying something *they* did not want to hear, canceling a valuable business meeting, walking away from a relationship that was all-important to the *other person*, or expressing beliefs and values that few appreciated or agreed with. Oh dear, it was so hard to disappoint other people!

Why? Because I grew up in a culture, a society, a family, and a church that gave message after message to support the concept, *the ideal*, of "agreement" — don't ripple the water; don't disappoint; don't ever do things most people do not subscribe to.

I went into the priesthood and became a fake. I was a fake because I said things I did not believe, in order to please the audience. I preached sermons that exhorted an ideal I had never subscribed to, for I knew the congregation loved it. I nodded at dinner parties when people espoused sexist and racist philosophies because I did not want to upset the apple cart. I even advised people in the confessional, who were clearly distraught and depressed, with directives the Church espoused, while I held out little comfort for the penitent. I was a fake.

I think I began to get *real* when I got sober. Something happened. I experienced a spiritual awakening that made me understand, at a deep level, that I could no longer live my life people-pleasing. There were times I needed to disappoint. Oh my God, how there were times I needed to disappoint!

As a priest, I wrote books about religious abuse and religious addiction. I said what I have always believed — there are many paths to God. I argued against racial and sexist intolerance, stating it revealed our own insecurities. I moved against my people-pleasing background when I said spirituality is not about being nice, but about being *real*!

I suddenly began to disappoint, and I felt good. Real. Spiritual. Not because I believed I was right, but because, for the first time in my life, I was saying what I believed. Thanks be to God!

PRAYER

I believe when I have the freedom to disappoint,
I am _real_.

I first heard this at a conference I attended. Initially I thought it was funny; later it stuck me as sad; then I thought, "Wow, this is *really* how some people think!" It's almost like the codependent is invisible, not a real entity, but an empty ghost—nothingness with a face! How do you *let go* of something that is not really there?

I suppose this is the ultimate in low self-esteem, the progression of loving others on a daily basis, and cutting off something of ourselves with each new love, and each new day. This sentence reveals a *death* in life: "When I'm home alone, nobody's there."

Where do we begin to heal? Obviously we need to remove and throw out the tapes in our heads that tell us others are more important; that we are empty without the love of another; and whatever *less than* means, we are it.

How? With affirmations repeated on a daily basis and supported by loving family and friends:

• *I am not only lovable, I am powerful.*

- *God's beauty shines through my presence.*

- *When I look into the mirror I see beauty and miracles looking back at me.*

- *I have few limitations and great possibilities.*

Also, I would suggest:

- *Attending codependent support groups, with the purpose and intention of healing the wounds and following directions.*

- *Spending time with a sponsor or friend whose journey to recovery you perceive as helpful.*

- *Affirming: Willingness = Action;*

  Healing = Belief in Self;

  Joy = Loving Presence.

All the above put flesh on our bones and help create a *presence*. We do not exist because other people see or enjoy us; we exist because we are. In our presence, God's existence is affirmed!

PRAYER

*Today, when I go home, before I switch on the TV,
call a friend, or get on the telephone, I go to the mirror
and say, "Wherever I am, God is!"*

Jesus said, "Love God and love our neighbor as ourselves."
You know, I never really heard the part about the need
to love ourselves!

It's strange, but we can hear the same sentence a thousand times, yet miss a key ingredient in it. As I've said throughout this book, a serious issue that shapes our dysfunctional thinking is religious addiction and religious abuse. Certainly this is true if we are to understand codependency. I'm not alone in saying my church upbringing gave me the message, covertly, that to be a good Christian I needed to forgive and love *other* people, and it was *decidedly selfish* for me to love myself. Only arrogant and self-centered people were seen as loving themselves; they liked themselves far too much!

Today I'm learning to let go of that message because it has proven to be very unhealthy in my life. How can I love other people if I don't have a healthy and energized love, on a daily basis, for myself? How can I really love and appreciate God if I don't have a love and appreciation for what God has made?

I do not say the Church told me I must *not* love myself, but the understanding I derived from my education in the congregation, and later in seminary, was that the main goal for the Christian was *sacrifice*. I must find a heavy cross and carry it. I must "die unto myself" to live more fully and spiritually for others. This is what I was told God wanted from me. The saints, the martyrs, and the men and women who were revered in Church history were those who sacrificed themselves for others. I never heard the message:

• *God wants you to love and appreciate your mind, body, and emotions.*

• *God is happy when you do good things for yourself.*

• *God knows you love yourself when you avoid unhealthy and dangerous people, and create healthy boundaries among your family and friends.*

• *God does not want you to burn yourself out at thirty-three trying to help those who do not want help.*

• *Only when you are able to give to yourself are you truly able to give to others.*

I did not heard these important statements because they were never spoken! Love of self was sinful. Today I'm able to love and do good things in my life *for me*, and everyone benefits. Burnout need not be part of the spiritual life!

PRAYER

God, I'm finding so much more to love about You as I take care of my needs. I'm empowered by Your spiritual energy when I love myself as part of Your glorious creation.

My low self-esteem was about living to please others.

It all seems so obvious now, but I can remember the time when I always, I mean always, placed other people before me. Other people's ideas were more important than mine; other people's needs came before mine. *I was a watering can for other people!*

I grew up in a family that loved me in many ways, but ours was a critical home, critical of me. I was blamed for many things I did not say or do. Other people were believed before I was believed. If a neighbor complained about something I had allegedly done, I got a good spanking.

Once when my friend broke a window with a ball, a neighbor noticed me and complained to my mother. I told her it was not me who threw the ball, but I was blamed, and I got the spanking!

I suppose at some point, if you are blamed and criticized enough, you believe it. You begin to doubt yourself. How could your parents be wrong? They would not punish you if you were a good boy. A strange thing

The Wisdom of Letting Go

begins to happen, unconsciously, and even though you know you are innocent, you still *believe* you are to blame!

In my early teenage years I grew to distrust, nay, *dislike* me, and I believed others were better. I began to like other people more than I liked myself. But I also wanted to be liked, so I started the people-pleasing routine that nearly killed me.

It only stopped when I began my recovery from alcoholism. When I attended group meetings, I discovered that not only was I lovable, but I was loved. Many people told me I did good things, and I wasn't always in the wrong. They pointed out while I may not have been perfect, I was very special — to God and to them! They told me I needed to make amends to Leo, write a love letter to Leo. I did, and I cried with happiness.

Today I want to please people, but I do not live to please people. However, I do live to please me. Only when I do good things for me am I truly able to do good and meaningful things for others, and God is happy.

PRAYER

God, I woke up very early the other night because I could not sleep, and I looked in the mirror and said, "I love you." Then I heard the dawn chorus. They agreed with me. I was ready for the day.

My children are not my possessions.

A woman spoke to me after I complimented the excellent behavior and manners of her two children. She thanked me, then said, "You know, Fr. Leo, these two beautiful children are gifts from God. They are free spirits. They are not my possessions."

It was a powerful moment for me because I realized then, in a most special way, how we cause damage in our relationships when we treat other people as our personal possessions. We do not own other people. They are truly free spirits.

* *They do not always do what we want them to do.*

* *They do not always speak or act in ways we want them to.*

* *They make decisions and often have opinions that infuriate us.*

Because... *they are not us*!

There is a form of codependency I detect in my life that is about ownership. I sometimes act as if I control other people, or that they have a duty in life to please me. It's an egotistical attitude I do not like about myself and I strive, on a daily basis, to heal this attitude.

Of course, it is about neediness — my neediness. If I were more secure in myself I would not need other people to do, act, speak, or behave the way I want. I would be able to live with their individuality.

My insecurity stems from the fact that I have a need to be right at all times. My way is the only way. It probably has something to do with the way I was raised. It certainly has something to do with the priesthood. But I know, today, it is not healthy.

Family and friends are gifts from God. I will enjoy them more, and get far more from them, when I allow them the freedom I demand for myself.

• *Only in freedom are there surprises.*

• *Only when we allow people their space can we be truly loved.*

• *Only when we recognize God's gift of free spirit can we appreciate art and diversity.*

We are not created the same. Thank God. What a wonderful world this is when I stop trying to control it, and everybody in it.

PRAYER

Great Spirit, I recognize Your freedom at the heart of creation and I thank You for the gift of diversity and difference.

My recovery involves seeing beyond the words,
into the action.

One aspect of my codependency is a reluctance to dig deeply into what people say. As a people-pleaser, I also want to be pleased. Often I take as face value what people say without looking for the corresponding action that should match the statement.

Why? I don't like disagreements. I want peace at any price. It's uncomfortable for me to hear arguments or to say I am displeased by a person's actions or behavior.

Coming from a dysfunctional family, where there were fights, arguments, sarcasm, and rageful expressions, I simply seek peace — peace at any price. But this is not always healthy, as there is often a price! Life cannot be about avoiding painful situations. Sometimes you must confront what people say, especially if it is not in spiritual alignment with an action. Tough love involves tough choices.

I am understanding today that I am not only expected to be responsible for what I say or do, I have a responsibility to *confront* others. Confront not in an angry or shaming way, but a spiritual confrontation that has expectations because of the relationship. It is not my goal to be weak, timid, or fearful of others. I do not want to be a coward who walks away from painful situations just because they are painful or awkward. If I expect an alignment from myself between words and action, then I should also expect that from family, friends, and colleagues.

Some subtle aspects of codependency are:

• *Avoidance.*

• *Walking away.*

• *Not rippling the waters.*

• *Peace at any price.*

• *Forgiving the unacceptable without asking for an amends.*

• *Allowing myself to be used.*

Today I expect the words to match the actions. I believe words are an aspect of divine energy, and should not be compromised. I do not intend to be a codependent people-pleaser who allows dysfunction and chaos to reign.

PRAYER

Lord, You are the word of truth, walking the path of righteousness. I seek to follow.

Today I'm choosing to be among positive people
who embrace balance.

Some years ago, a mantra echoed through my mind which I have since found to be useful on a daily basis: Spirituality = being positive and creative.

When I look around at the spiritual people I admire, they are invariably most positive in their approach to life and creative in the way they seek to live and communicate with others. Jesus Christ is a supreme example, but there are many non-Christians who also live the spiritual lifestyle.

When I think about my codependency, I can see I was a negative and destructive person, not willing to embrace change. I always wanted to live the easier and softer way, which was not actually easier, or softer. It was too much trouble to change my behavior, and confront attitudes in myself that were harmful. I was lazy about my affect and my language. I did not nurture the creative spirit within. I had exchanged the Kingdom of God for a waterless desert!

Also, my codependency led me into the company of many who were equally helpless and visionless—

The Wisdom of Letting Go

procrastinators and no-sweat type people. I was not happy.

This has not been my lifestyle for many years now because I experienced a spiritual awakening. My pain made me contemplate "gain." I was *more*, much more than the way I was living. I embraced the spiritual concept, expressed in my mantra, of being a positive and creative *human-being*. Living in the God Zone.

This has led me to find friends and colleagues who are also positive and creative. They need not be Christian, and they need not believe all I believe. We can agree to disagree, as long as we walk a spiritual path.

• *We treated ourselves and others with respect.*

• *We viewed life as an adventure, not an endurance test.*

• *We sought to heal, on a daily basis, our bodies, minds, and emotions with positive affirmations.*

• *We believed God was at work in our lives.*

Balance was the goal of this lifestyle.

PRAYER

Because I believe You are at work in my life, and I know You to be a positive and creative energy, so I seek to be the spiritual optimist.

I will survive.

I believe it is easier to be good than evil. I believe it is easier to be sober than drunk. I believe it is easier to tell the truth than live the life of a liar. I believe it is easier to love than hate. These beliefs will take me through the door of death, into eternal life. *I will survive.*

I've not always believed this. I had to let go of some very old tapes that affirmed the opposite, because those old tapes only made my life difficult:

- *It is hard to stop drinking.*
- *It is hard to tell the truth.*
- *It is hard to love people.*
- *It is hard to speak your mind.*
- *It is hard to establish boundaries.*
- *It is hard to walk away from an unhealthy relationship.*
- *It is hard to "tough love" your kids.*

On and on those old tapes went. For years I believed them. I kept playing those old tapes in my head, and I lived my life accordingly. Then somebody confronted me: "Are they true?" I realized they were not true, only repetitive!

• *It is very hard to remain a drunk. Life is much easier when you put down the bottle.*

• *It is easier to tell the truth. Then you wake up each day knowing what you need to say – the truth.*

• *Only when we love people will we get and appreciate love.*

• *Once you begin to speak your mind, let go of people-pleasing. Then people soon learn what to expect – honesty.*

• *Only with boundaries are you able to live creatively, without the feeling of suffocation.*

• *Walking away from a painful relationship allows for the possibility of new relationships.*

• *Tough love allows your children to recognize you really are their parent, not just their friend.*

When I was willing to change the tapes, my life became easier because I moved over to God's side. Survival in the company of God is never difficult.

PRAYER

When I recognize the power of God's true message in my mind, I am able to make the survival choices that lead to success.

Spirituality

Chapter 3

I love you enough to let you go.

I define spirituality as being a positive and creative human being. It's difficult being spiritual if you are constantly unhappy. And who among us would want to let go of something that is making us happy, joyous, and free?

We let go of those things that are holding us back:

- *A relationship that is not working out.*

- *A belief system that does not resonate with our soul.*

- *A friendship that is one-sided.*

- *A family so dysfunctional it has become a nightmare to stay involved.*

- *A childhood relationship with God that has grown into childishness.*

Spirituality has never been about being nice! I'm using the word "nice" to imply ingratiating behavior that is so often fake and comes close to hypocrisy.

Oh no, spirituality is always about being real!

This is why so many people find it difficult to let a person go — because they don't want to be unkind, seem ungrateful, or disappoint. Little do they realize how much of their spiritual power they have given away by this *dysfunctional nicety*.

Let's be *really* clear — spirituality is about God. It is about reflecting God's power, God's energy, and God's concern for righteousness. For these reasons, the spiritual person will often walk alone.

PRAYER

I am willing to let go of those people who suffocate my spirituality. I'm no longer prepared to exist in a relationship that is not soul-enhancing.

Spirituality is about being positive and creative;
today I know I have the power to let go of
those things that are destroying me.

In the Twelve Step program, at the twelfth step, we hear the phrase: "Having had a spiritual awakening..." Something has happened. A moment of realization dawns. The penny drops, the ice breaks, we are made to *see*. To see what? That we have *power*.

The spiritual path is not about remaining a victim of life, powerless, with an unmanageable existence. Rather, spirituality is the path to God's power, and has already been given to us.

We do not have to get spirituality. We must discover spirituality within our very nature.

God's energy is linked to the Kingdom within. For too long, people who involve themselves in Twelve Step programs realize how they have missed themselves by selling themselves short, and believing alcohol, sex, food, or other people had the power while they themselves were less than. Then the moment of awakening dawns: "I am a swan. I'm not just an ugly duckling."

With this realization, a new life is born. We become responsible. The metaphysical understanding of co-creation is discovered when we place our hand in the hand of God.

God is beckoning us to a new world order and we need to *respond*.

• *We say goodbye to destructive behavior.*

• *Goodbye to a negative lifestyle.*

• *Goodbye to victim thinking.*

• *Goodbye to people whose behavior epitomizes unmanageability and powerlessness.*

• *Goodbye to a "fix-it" God who can only deliver smoke and mirrors.*

We realize the miracle of the spiritual awakening is not so much that we love God, but that we have begun to *love ourselves*.

PRAYER

Today I am aware God is inviting me to a co-creative dance, and sometimes I am expected to lead.

Spirituality is not about having everything together;
it is about knowing one day I want to be-together.

I'm not perfect. I'm not God. I don't have to have everything together. It's okay to make mistakes. It seems strange to write this because it all seems so obvious when it's in black and white. Why do I need to tell myself I'm not God?

Yet sometimes, I *feel* as if I should be perfect, as if I should have everything together, and I *feel* guilty when I make mistakes. And when I feel like this, I'm *playing God*.

Spirituality entails the concept of acceptance. Not simply the acceptance of others, but also a real acceptance of ourselves — warts and all!

Spirituality is the healing balm for guilt and shame because it always beckons us to a new day, and new opportunities. It picks us up and dusts us off. And we need this.

Why do we need this? Because we all make mistakes, and rarely does a day pass without our doing, saying, or thinking something we regret:

The Wisdom of Letting Go

- *The stupid lie that makes no sense.*

- *The thoughtless remark that created pain for somebody we love.*

- *The ongoing procrastination around what we need to accomplish.*

- *Destructive thoughts that occur in the most innocent of settings.*

- *The hypocrisy of our behavior that we love and hate, all at the same time.*

This is life, everyone's life.

The saints are examples not because they are perfect, but because they know *they are not*. Who among us cannot identify with St. Augustine's prayer: "Lord give me chastity… but not yet."

Spirituality understands this. And spirituality energizes us to be better, healthier, and more forgiving of ourselves.

We press on to be "more together!"

PRAYER

Dear God, I do not pray for You to accept my failings, because I know You do; I pray I might accept my failings. Spirituality is a synonym for letting go.

The disciple asked the master:
"Why do I find it so hard to walk life's path?"
The master replied instantly:
"Because you carry things you do not need."

I've read so many spiritual books over the years, and they all seem to have in common a recurring central theme: "Keep it simple."

I suppose it is impossible to keep life simple and uncluttered without the willingness to let some things go.

• *Do we really need all the religious law and dogma?*

• *Most of the things we fear in life will never happen.*

• *When we ask a friend what they enjoy about us, it is often the thing we didn't work very hard to develop.*

• *Nothing we accumulate and collect will last.*

If we really wish to experience the spiritual life, we need to have the willingness to unpack our baggage, and leave some of it behind!

It does not make sense to do what most of us seem to be doing — that is, unpacking baggage only to fill up again with even more!

Who am I? I'm a child of God.
What am I? A spiritual being in human form.
Where am I going? Home.

PRAYER

Today I know if I am to reach my destination,
I need to let go of those things that hold me down.

Only when I let go do I know I belong.

It has often been said in Zen philosophy that we need to die in life in order to live. Paradox. The above statement is a similar paradox.

We let go in order to create a meaningful space that allows for understanding and growth. Spirituality is surely involved in this type of paradox because we cannot explain fully what it means to be a spiritual person. Spirituality is in itself a living paradox because it seeks to hold together heaven and Earth, the infinite and the finite, yesterday and tomorrow, while truly living in the present.

We let go in order to belong. How can this be?

One explanation is that we cease to control our destiny in the sense of ownership, and move to the place where we can *experience* each moment as a sense of adventure. Our sense of belonging comes in knowing we are part of this adventure, and this stimulates our creativity.

Although we need to be responsible for our lives, we all realize we cannot *control* life because things happen

The Wisdom of Letting Go

that are beyond ourselves. Accidents happen, people do things we do not expect, and events occur in nature that may throw us a curve. We can react, and must react, but we do not *control*. If we were to try to be responsible for all that happens to us in life, we would drive ourselves crazy.

In what sense, then, can we say we belong? Our sense of belonging comes in knowing these things are not just happening to us, but they are happening to everyone.

We can have a bad day. We all know what it is like to have somebody let us down or create pain; we have all experienced *helplessness* in life, because these are universal experiences. In this sense, we *belong*.

We need not see ourselves as victims, for there is not some cosmic plot to upset our plans or dreams, and the world does not hold a grudge! In a very spiritual sense, the act of letting go creates an expression of belonging — we are not alone.

PRAYER
*Today I let go in order to be at one with
myself and the universe.*

Spirituality melts the rigidity of
so much religious thought.

Rigid thought can be abusive because it does not allow for creativity or change. Black and white thinking — this is how it ought to be, it was good enough for those who came before us and it should be good enough for us, who gives you the right to change our traditions — all such attitudes create a suffocating box with its lid screwed tight!

Nowhere is this more toxic than when such thinking is applied to religion:

• *The Bible says it so God commands it.*

• *The Church is not an institution of change.*

• *Religion does not exist to accommodate us, but seeks to obey God.*

• *There is no excuse for breaking God's word.*

• *The path to Hell is built through non-religious choices.*

We all come across people who reflect the above religious thinking and they all have one thing in common: *they believe — nay, they know — they are right!*

I've written extensively in my other books about religious abuse. It exists in a kind of celestial arrogance, a belief that there is only one way to God, only one understanding of God's word, and the notion that God does not allow for an evolution in religious thought.

All the great religions have their fanatics, and those are usually literalists. They rarely appreciate poetic and figurative language, and they loathe and fear *situational interpretation.*

For example: it is not "un-Christian" to interpret Jesus' words, "Nobody can come to the Father except by Me," within an inclusive philosophy, i.e., the "me" of the sentence might be "the path of truth and righteousness" we experience in the life and teaching of Mahatma Gandhi!

Spirituality always seeks to melt "frozen thinking" into a fluid inclusiveness based on respect and dignity for all people, including their religions.

PRAYER

God of Oneness, may I continue to comprehend You in the diversity of Your creation.

I truly believe God is not a controlling codependent, for God has let go of creation in freedom. We are free to join the spiritual path, or we are free to destroy.

I believe this says something wonderful about God because in the act of letting go is our dignity and co-creativity.

- *We are not puppets on a string.*
- *Our happiness is determined by our lifestyle.*
- *Spirituality celebrates the miracle of choice and responsibility.*
- *The act of letting go is implicit in our creation, hence the history of human kind.*
- *Greatness has no meaning without freedom.*

This, then, is the divine model.

God's nature is to create that spiritual space, the *let go zone*, where we can experience freedom in all its totality: the good and the bad, the healing and the abusive, the shame and the self-forgiveness, and the violence and the healing.

PRAYER

Great Spirit, I hear Your cry, "Let go."
I experience Your detached loving energy,
and I respond: "Thy will be done."

Spirituality is looking at a leaking bucket,
knowing it will never become empty.

God's love will never drain away. We can never exhaust the justice that exists at the heart of God. Divine energy will never cease.

Spirituality is the leaking bucket that will never empty. What does this metaphor say to us?

• *We can drink from this bucket of life.*

• *The good flows into our lives.*

• *The spiritual principle of "letting go" is an ingredient of this flow.*

• *Created in the image of God, we will never become empty.*

The key to this spiritual awareness is *looking*. If we do not look, we will never see. This is the all-important co-creative act, and without it, we will never have any *real* success.

So many people are deluded into thinking, often because of religious abuse, that God will do everything and they need only surrender to "His" will, and success is a gift that requires no move from ourselves. These teachings are spiritually erroneous!

"Having eyes do you not see; ears do you not hear."

We need to turn *our* attention to *our* part in creating success.

- *We need to look.*
- *We need to turn in a new direction.*
- *We need to change.*
- *We need to actively hear the word of God, then act on that word.*
- *We need to take responsibility for our part in creating miracles.*

As with all metaphors, all figurative language, the comprehension of their spiritual meaning lies within ourselves.

What does the leaking bucket mean to you?

PRAYER

*I am at one with the ever-flowing spirit of God
which will never dry up.*

I know I am apart; yet spirituality also tells me
I am involved.

An aspect of letting go is knowing not only are we not God, but we cannot have all the answers to life's puzzling situations. We know only in part. Only through death will we see face to face.

With this in mind, we cannot explore the spiritual life without the use of paradox—saying two things at the same time that seem contradictory.

We are apart, yet we are involved. I think all of us know this to be true on a feeling level. We sense we are separate from other people. Even the people who really love us do not fully know us.

Words can help in communicating what we are thinking and feeling, but they cannot comprehensively explain our totality.

Having said this, we also know and feel we are involved, connected, at-one-with. We are not completely separated from our fellow and sister human beings. We feel what they feel. We often share thoughts they have experienced. Life creates involvement.

We all must live this paradox. St. Augustine said it this way: "We are restless until we rest in God."

Maybe the restlessness is the odd fusion created by our being apart, while being involved.

PRAYER

Dear God, I know at times I feel apart,
yet I know I am involved.

Spirituality is not about forgiving the past.
That is relatively easy. It's about forgiving, period!

Nearly every book written about spirituality includes the concept of forgiveness. Forgiveness is the process often linked with living the spiritual life.

Why? Because without forgiveness — not just the forgiveness of others, but the forgiveness of ourselves — we live in a prison.

The walls are anger, resentment, blame, and victimization:

• *Anger: We are angry about something a person has done or said, and if we are not able to forgive, we stay stuck in the moment of abuse.*

• *Resentment: We are unable to be in the same company as the person we feel has hurt us without being sarcastic, aloof, or passive-aggressive.*

• *Blame: We cannot move beyond the incident because we are forever pointing our finger at the other person. It is their fault!*

• *Victimization: Although we may feel we are the innocent party, we are still the victim, unable to experience the freedom that comes with letting go.*

Forgiveness is a living spiritual quality that needs to be practiced in the present so we may continue to be positive and creative in our lives. Only when we forgive can we move beyond the prison of anger, resentment, blame, and victimization. Forgiveness is freedom.

Prayer
Today I refuse to stay a prisoner of past hurts.
I forgive, and let go. I move beyond the abuse.

I don't believe in God, Jesus, or the Church.
But in a strange way, I believe I am spiritual.

For many years I have underscored the difference between being religious and being spiritual. It would be strange to say you were religious but didn't believe in God, Jesus, or the Church. But spirituality is something different. Spirituality recognizes an "otherness" in creation that involves energy, mingled with a *poetic love* for humanity. I've described it as a golden thread that unites all human beings, affirming their inherent goodness. A spiritual person is also positive and creative in life.

Not a few people who say they are spiritual rather than religious have also experienced religious abuse. For example, when they were growing up, they may have experienced the Church as rigid, narrow, judgmental, and boring. They simply never, not even as children, felt any connection to what the Church asked them to read, or what clergy taught from the pulpit.

Some people were abused in a more overt manner, e.g., women and gays, experiencing from an early age what they felt was a lack of hospitality on the part of Christianity. They left. Period.

I'm often quick to remind people the Church has abused many in its long history, but in recent years, say the last twenty, it has gone through a major reevaluation of its past attitudes, and a healing has begun. I'm very comfortable in the Episcopal Church and, although at times I feel it is a tad stuffy, I can live with it.

I'm convinced if people who left the Church twenty years ago were to revisit the Church today, they would find, in many cases, considerable changes for the better have taken place. Maybe we all need to let go of the past and begin this new millennium celebrating change and diversity.

For me, Jesus was a victim of religious abuse because the religion of his birth moved against him when he suggested reinterpreting scriptures, e.g., "You have heard what was said to you of old times, but I say unto you..." It could be argued the Church is the natural home for the religious critic!

Prayer
I am understanding, Lord, that spirituality is beyond words, form, and ritual; it is a place that welcomes and nurtures everyone.

*Spirituality is the freedom to see beyond
the religious box.*

When I wrote *The God Game: It's Your Move*, I included a chapter on the "God Box," which figuratively is the container of unhealthy religious attitudes and statements:

• *You must obey the Church if you are to go to Heaven.*

• *Jesus is the only way to salvation.*

• *God watches and punishes all the people who do evil; often the sins are visited on the children.*

• *Homosexuals are child abusers and will roast in the fires of Hell.*

• *A Christian woman makes for an obedient wife.*

• *The Bible is God's instruction book that will get you into Heaven.*

• *People are healed as they come closer to God.*

Of course, we have all experienced other unhealthy phrases and attitudes as we grew up, but my "God Box" is filled with the above. It was so frustrating and claustrophobic that I nearly left the Church. How could so many apparently nice people say such terrible things? But they did.

At a critical point in my life, I read about spirituality and saw there was a "kinder face" to religion. It was a refrain based upon spiritual principles, not simply religious dogma. Gandhi summed it up beautifully when he said, "An eye for an eye makes the whole world blind."

If we insist on staying rooted in the fundamentalist religious word, we will become inflexible religious abusers. But if we allow the light of spirituality to shine on our text, we will become reconcilers.

I believe freedom is dear to the heart of God, and the reality of creation is its inherent diversity. Therefore to compare, contrast, and *condemn* is a mission to chaos.

PRAYER
You have given us in the same scriptures the key
to open our individual "God Box."
May I have the courage to use it.

*Jesus is only alive if we are willing
to look beyond the cross.*

It is possible for a Christian to be a spiritual person if she or he is willing to see the "gospel" in a larger context than simply the history of the Church. It is important to move beyond suffering into abundance, beyond an emphasis upon what we are not into the co-creative experience of who we are, and beyond limitation to resurrected possibilities.

As a Christian, when I say Jesus is alive, I am referring to the ongoing relationship I have with His message. It is a message that should not be defined in Church-controlled dogma. Jesus is that free spirit who constantly surprises.

As a young man growing up, I was surrounded in the Church building with statues of suffering, men and women who were tortured for their faith. This is certainly an important aspect of understanding the development of Christianity, but it is not the *most important* message.

Abuse comes with overemphasis. If we remain focused on the suffering, we will remain victims. We need to be pointed toward resurrection, glory, new life, limitless possibilities, hope, and transformation.

We really do miss the miracle of Jesus if we remain on the cross. We should be willing to supplement our own scriptures with the spiritual inspiration of poets, writers, painters, musicians, and the religious experiences characteristic of *other* faiths. We must not make our God too small.

PRAYER

I see my possibilities enshrined in the new life
Jesus birthed into this world.
So long as we continue to dream,
it will never die.

Only when I was willing to let go of religion did I discover spirituality.

This book is about letting go, which in turn is about synchronicity. It is about bringing things together, looking at them in a different way, creating ideas not usually associated with religious words, and seeing through a different pair of spectacles.

This is certainly true in the way I am suggesting we approach the phrase "letting go." A literal interpretation would mean we discard, remove from our custody, or dispense with something, some issue. But that is not what I mean when I say, "let go." Rather, I mean approach the phrase creatively, don't overemphasize, but be willing to contemplate other ideas and opinions, and to embrace paradox.

Spirituality is the most important concept in my life, but I have not removed myself from religion. In many cases I am grateful to my religious heritage for feeding my mind with the essence of my spiritual building blocks. I needed to move beyond the security of my early black-and-white thinking in order to embrace a spirituality that was more inclusive. I needed to let go of crisp definitions in order to appreciate subtlety. Shades and shadows make up the spiritual life.

I needed to play in my relationship with God, rather than stay obediently on my knees. The child of God needed to grow up!

Religion is a little like the nest a young bird needs early in life but which, *in order to fly*, it must eventually leave behind. We, too, must move beyond the nest. We need to risk.

PRAYER

Dear God, I am more than words can ever define.

And so is my faith.

Healthy memories are the ones we are able to let go.

For many years I was trapped in my memories. I was unable to move forward in my life because I had built a shrine to the past.

Instead of visiting it occasionally with respect, I locked myself inside and threw away the key. I was a prisoner. My memories had become my life.

- *Spending valuable time only thinking of the past.*

- *Not going out just in case that person telephoned.*

- *Avoiding significant relationships that had great potential because I felt guilty and disloyal.*

- *Talking about change but fearing risk.*

- *Missing the miracle of the moment because of the morbid revisiting of the past.*

These memories are killers. We either move beyond them, or we will atrophy — and die.

- *Healthy memories are the ones we can revisit at our leisure, then get on with the present, enjoying the moment.*

- *Healthy memories do not move into our lives and take us hostage.*

• *Healthy memories do not linger.*

• *Healthy memories are not offended when we say to them, "Enough already! It was nice remembering, but I have other things in my life."*

• *Healthy memories are the ones we are able to let go.*

Because spirituality is about being positive and creative, we all need to guard against the codependent memories that make us victims.

PRAYER

God, I am understanding that I value my memories

only when I cease to enshrine them in a present reality.

It is an insult to Your new day to linger in the past.

Embracing spirituality is really about the adventure
of letting go.

When we really come down to it, spirituality is about knowing we have the freedom to achieve great things, and need not sweat the small stuff. It is striving for the big picture, rather than staying closeted in religious dogma or holy books that work, *but not for everyone*!

There will always be people who believe Jesus is the only way, homosexuality is a sin, the Bible is the only revelation from God, or the world will end on Monday evening—before *Ally McBeal!* These extreme positions will always exist. However, there is a growing number of people who feel a connection with a gentler, more inclusive and compassionate spirit—spirituality.

In our society we see more and more people who are letting go of "old" religion in order to embrace and experience the "new" age. Petition has been nurtured by co-creation!

Spirituality is an adventure that carries responsibility. It is not sufficient to kneel before a statue, say a few Hail Marys, and ask God to grant our request. Oh no, now we need to be *involved* in what it is we are requesting. Ready to do the footwork.

Many very religious people who are recovering alcoholics tend to suggest they would not be sober had it not been for their Higher Power, God, or Jesus. This would be a *conservative* religious position.

I, on the other hand, tend to emphasize the spiritual path by pointing out that I'm sober today because *I did* things differently. I went to support meetings. I entered the hospital. I put down the bottle.

Believing in God, reading the Bible, and praying to Jesus, didn't stop me when I was drinking!

God, of course, wants alcoholics sober, but they *need* to want it too.

PRAYER

God, You have given me the power to determine my life.
Today I appreciate the responsibility You have
shared with me.

I ask: "Do You love me?"

God asks: "Do you love Me enough to let go?"

Sometimes I sit in the kitchen and imagine all manner of conversations God and I are having. The above is an example of such a dialogue.

I don't know what you think about this. Indeed, I would love to hear from you, and I can tell you what came to me during this dialogue:

• *God is seeking space from my constant "begging" intercessions.*

• *God is telling me to move out of the "holy nest" I pad with religious texts and paraphernalia.*

• *God is reminding me I was created to create, not stagnate.*

• *God is echoing the words of Kahlil Gibran: "Let there be space in our togetherness."*

• *God hates enmeshment and demands respectful detachment.*

So often, when we read about what letting go means, the reference is to letting go of control so we can place our lives at the feet of God. To avoid *playing God*, we need to hand over our lives to God's care.

But I think there is also a twist.

God is also saying to us, "Don't keep hanging onto me. Don't cling. *Let go and live.*"

Truly, spirituality is the healing agent for codependency because it emphasizes a God-given energy that exists in all of us that *needs* — oh how it needs — to be activated. The abused peoples of the world need to give their prayers feet. Only then will they experience miracle.

PRAYER

Great Spirit, You demand from Your children the courage to move out of the safety zone into the challenging space of creativity.

The disciple asked,
"What do I need to know in order to become spiritual?"
The Master replied,
"Let go of what you think you know."

The longer I live, the more I realize how much I fail to understand.

- *Life really is a mystery. A spiritual mystery.*

- *In order to find God, we must know God is within.*

- *The Jesus who called us to listen has also been listening.*

- *The more we seek to control, the less responsibility we have.*

- *The sinner is often the saint with a human face.*

- *The rich complain, while the poor appreciate the song from a bird in the field.*

- *Less is more; and more is never enough.*

I'm sure I'm not alone in realizing I missed the *fragrance* and energy of spirituality because I carried so much religious baggage.

I had learned the rules, and knew the catechism. I had studied the Bible, and understood the import of the sacred councils.

But still I did not understand.

W. H. Davies says it beautifully:

> *What is the life*
> *If full of care,*
> *We have no time*
> *To stand and stare.*

I need to *see* the roses before I can I stop and smell them.

PRAYER

Mysterious Spirit, I'm glad You made Life in Your confusing image. This way, I don't feel so alone in my confusion.

The spiritual understanding of letting go
includes responsibility.

Because I have witnessed the pain of religious addiction and abuse, I'm very sensitive to the dangers of believing letting go means handing our lives, goals, dreams, relationships, or finances over to God, expecting God to take care of everything.

I heard somebody say recently: "I need to get out of the driver's seat and let God take control." This man was facing bankruptcy. He is now bankrupt. He is also angry at God for not doing a good job!

Excuse me, please. What has happened to an appreciation of poetry and word-drama? Why do we need to take letting go so literally? Of course it involves:

• *Trust*	• *Change*
• *Prayer*	• *Grace*
• *Faith*	• *Hope*

But it also involves *RESPONSIBILITY*.

God did not create this world to be dependent. God gave the world freedom.

From this gift of freedom evolved the world you and I find ourselves in today:

- *We may not like it, but it's here.*
- *We may wish things were different, but they're not.*
- *We can complain, but that achieves nothing.*

The alternative is to do what all successful people do and that is, metaphorically, place our hand in the hand of God, and start to look for a spade. God will hold one hand but requires the other hand to be free. We need a free hand to pick up the spade!

PRAYER

God, I know today I'm willing, ready, and able.
I know You are, also. This is a great partnership.

Separation

Chapter 4

I know I've done the right thing,
but it feels so painful.

It is not always easy to do the right thing. Just because something is right, that does not make it easy. We often wish we could do the "right thing" a different way, without an argument, without separation. That is a fantasy that will keep us feeling miserable. It's never easy to separate from the one we love. Why do we have to do it? First of all, we don't *have* to do it. We don't *have* to do anything. We could keep everything the same, and keep getting the same old results.

Why do we do it? Because we want to live, to move away from the pain. We would rather face the loneliness of tomorrow than stay in the pain of today. Separation is part of the *tough love* we give ourselves. To experience happiness, we now require an *action* — separation.

Separation is always the answer to abuse. We must be prepared to let go of messages that suggest:

• *Everything will work out in the end.*

• *You are simply carrying your cross. Salvation is in the next life.*

• *God is in charge of your life. Get out of the driver's seat!*

- *Things are the way they are supposed to be.*
- *We got married (for better or worse) and we must live with it.*
- *No one ever said you were supposed to be happy.*

We have a myriad messages that need to be examined and interpreted, and not accepted at face value. Separation is not easy, but may be desirable. Sometimes separation creates healing. When we take a step back from the relationship, both people get a chance to be objective. And maybe, just maybe, we can come back together with a different set of tapes, a different set of rules, and a different (more healthy) lifestyle.

A friend separated from her husband because he was disinterested and antisocial. She loved him, but was dying inside. They both went to codependency meetings. She was surprised when she learned he went to therapy. The separation created the pain he needed to experience. He realized he had alienated the one he really loved, and had taken her for granted. He made amends. They began to see each other again–and actually dated. Their love was rekindled. They got back together. Miracle. Created by separation!

Sometimes it does not work out this way, but the necessary separation holds the possibility of spiritual self-love. And the pain, though it may never go away completely, begins to heal.

PRAYER

*Great Spirit, at times You have separated Yourself in love.
Now some of Your children must walk this path.*

Because I've felt the pain of abandonment so often,
when I hear the words, "I need to tell you something,"
I just go weak in the knees.

Life is not based upon what we need just for today; it is based upon how life really is.

People are afraid. They fear rejection. They fear being abandoned. They are really afraid because their lives have not been happy.

Alcoholism, drug addiction, sexual abuse—so many people have been affected by these issues. It's too much.

Life has a way of getting away from us.

In the sentence at the beginning of the story we hear, "I go weak in the knees." Why? I know why. We go weak in the knees because we are insecure. We hate to find people do not like us, love us, or care about us.

Abandonment is a real issue, and it is often about ourselves. This is not what we want to hear, but it is true.

Do we really know how people feel about us? When we talk about abandonment, do we really include ourselves?

But why go weak in the knees? Because we are lonely. We feel lost. There is no joy for the future.

So what do we do?

Well, we don't give up. We don't give way to feeling life is over. We certainly don't give up because we are separated. People have been known to come back together, and if they don't, they have a chance to find a new life.

Really, let's stop feeling sorry for ourselves. Life is to be lived.

PRAYER

God, I need You so much.

God bless me.

Stay with me while I find my strength.

When I left, I knew I would return.
But it would never be the same.

A friend once said that sometimes we must go in order to return. Separation. Letting go clearly applies to relationships, but the reactions and consequences are also true for job, school, country, and "childhood memories." We realize, after we have been away for a period of time, that it's *never quite the same*. When we make a move we always create a change. The change can be for good, or not so good — even bloody awful!

In the quest to love, it is sometimes essential that we move away and create a real separation in order to *improve* a relationship, not least the relationship with ourselves. The interesting part of the above statement is: "I knew I would return." This is an actual experience for me, and I've discovered many have had a similar experience — we sometimes leave a relationship knowing it is *not over.* In our minds we knowingly carry the words of General MacArthur, "I shall return." Is this codependency? Maybe. Are we not told when we move on we should not look back? No return. This may be true for many relationships, but certainly not for all!

Life is not easy, and relationships can be even harder. I knew when I walked away from one particular relationship, as I was saying (loudly), *"It's all over. Never again!"* I knew I would return, for in my heart I was not ready to go. It's a little like stopping smoking: we can mouth the words but something inside must *want* to stop. I did not want to leave. It was not over.

My separation was a form of intervention; although I knew I would return, *I also knew* it would never be the same. You cannot create separation without also creating change. Feelings will be different. History is interrupted. Words, real or exaggerated, have been exchanged. It will never be the same. At the time of this writing, I am no longer in that relationship. I returned only to go away again. I bet it sounds familiar. Through my conversations with people, alongside my own experience, I've learned there is a process of "going before we go." Separation is rarely a single event.

I do not regret the experience. I still love. For that time, at that time, it did not work. But notice, even as I write, a part of me knows it's not over. Love, relationship, intimate moments, I don't think ever really end. All we have is separation, and we do not know if it is permanent until death enters the drama!

PRAYER

I celebrate my co-creative act of separation that in so many ways helped create a healing in the relationship, even if the relationship did not last.

It seems I've spent my whole life separated
from someone.

There is an aspect of the spiritual life that must include separation, a personal aloneness that is not really good or bad, but simply *is*.

Although I have had wonderful relationships with many people, there is a part of me I know is separate; separate from other people, even from God. This is the grit in the pearl, the pearl of creativity.

Oftentimes it is those moments of aloneness that help me be the most productive, inspirational, and *aware*— aware that we will always be restless until we rest in God. There are times when I am with somebody and I know I do not fully understand them, and they do not fully understand me. My feelings, those reactions to life that feed my soul, are impossible to fully articulate and sometimes, even when I've used the finest words I can muster, I still am not fully represented, or fully known.

This *not being fully understood by another* has helped me really concentrate in the last few years on self-awareness and self-love because I realize the only person I can *really*

The Wisdom of Letting Go

understand, *really* experience, *really* connect with is myself. Because *I* don't have to explain my feelings, *I* feel them. *I* don't have to spend time writing down my thoughts, *I'm* thinking them. The pain and stresses that make up my life *I* know, because they are *mine*. *I* don't just live my life, *I* feel it.

For too long I spent my energy on either trying to fully understand another person, or getting them to fully understand me, and something was always missing. If I spend my whole life seeking to know and understand me, that will be enough. Also, today I accept the mystery that is necessarily at the heart of all relationships; indeed it is the *not knowing* that creates the passion, energy, daily suspense, and wonderment.

Maybe this feeling of *separateness* from God is what the early theologians tried to describe with the doctrine of The Fall. However, I feel the creative ingredient of our separateness got lost in the Church's heavy emphasis upon guilt and sin. Our separated restlessness from God feeds the energy of our co-creativeness. It is our use of this freedom that makes us Great. Noble. Saints.

PRAYER

I'm so aware of my aloneness.
But I believe it is somehow connected with my uniqueness,
my divine specialness.

Sometimes I feel an all-consuming desire to connect,
so I make the telephone call.
When they answer, I can't say a word.

Let's face it, separation from the people we love is painful. It's even more painful if someone we love, for whatever reason, is simply not good for us, and we have separated for our own well-being.

Then we weaken. Our thinking goes awry and we forget the reason we separated. We forget all the painful experiences, all the fights and quarrels, all the hardship, and we remember only the good times. *Stinking thinking* is really selective thinking, and the selection is not healthy.

So we make the call we said we would never make. Like the alcoholic who said he had put down the drink forever, then finds himself with a glass of beer in his hand; like the sex addict who said he would never read pornography again, then finds himself in the adult bookshop; so the pain and loneliness of separation drives the telephone call. And the person answers. Then our fear returns, and the horror of the relationship is remembered.

A moment of sanity. The head and heart combine to say, "I must not say a word."

It's hard to separate from somebody we have loved. We do not always love healthy people. Sometimes we love people we do not really like, or have little in common with. If somebody had described, years before we met, the kind of relationship we have been involved in, we would have sworn they were crazy.

On this occasion, the person has the courage not to speak. But it would have been better if they had never telephoned, because one day they could weaken, hear the voice, and respond. Then the sick cycle would begin again. The promises. The remembered happy times. The sorrowful tears. *Maybe we should try one more time!*

PRAYER

Great Spirit, I recognize I have desires
that could destroy me.
And I take responsibility for them.
Today I know my spiritual strength is
more powerful than my destructive desires.

Separation still involves connection.

When we have a strong friendship or love relationship with somebody, but feel we must separate — perhaps the person is self-destructive, or betrays us, or moves to another country and we lose contact — there is still a connection. I'm not talking about in a mere acquaintance, but in a friendship, or a deep love, something of the relationship never dies.

As I get older, I remember the many special people who have crossed my path, some of them thirty or forty years ago. Something is said, something happens, perhaps I have some free time and I'm reminiscing on my life, and they return. Memories.

Some of these memories are not necessarily happy — lost love, an argument, or a misunderstanding followed by separation. Yet, what are we but the sum total of our memories? Life's experiences invariably involve people. Some of these people are special in our minds and hearts, we have feelings about these people, and we've made *connection*.

We may never see these people again, or speak with them on the telephone, or write a letter, yet they have become part of us. We let them go, but a part of them remains.

When I was in college, I met many young men who were my contemporaries, studying for the priesthood. We argued together, laughed together, hurt, and at times let each other down. Then we separated. I've never seen most of them again.

Then I'll be looking for some papers in my library *thirty years later* and find a photograph, and those fellows return. And I return, just for a few moments, to my youth. The conversations, mannerisms, sarcasm, and love all return — *connection*. I'm happy.

PRAYER

Thank You for the variety of people who
have connected with me in life;
they have helped make me who I am.

Sometimes I wake up and smell you in the bed.

I miss you.

When you love somebody, really love somebody, and they are no longer with you, you miss them. It's as if part of your life has gone. Nothing seems the same.

What can you do? Romance is one thing, and if you are a committed romantic, you can spend the rest of your life smelling your lover in the sheets, or the wardrobe, and maybe even in the bathroom. But life needs to go on.

Notice I say life *needs* to go on; I didn't say it *must* go on. Many people die in their romance; the beloved leaves and life begins to fade. Some people find it hard to let go because they keep repeating in their minds that it is *hard to let go*. But isn't it harder to die in life? Isn't it harder to place your life so completely in the hands of another that you become a "thing," a puppet that allows others to pull the strings?

Staying home, not answering the phone, refusing to attend parties, drawing the curtains in your house, and refusing to go out--now that is hard!

Of course we must go through a grieving stage when we separate from somebody we love, but practicality tells us *life needs to go on*. We must begin to respect ourselves, begin nurturing life again, meeting new and exciting people.

At some point we must let go and say "Yes" to life–our life!

We need the new tape in our minds that says our life is not about other people, but what we are willing to create.

We need new affirmations that empower us:

- *I am more than the people I love.*
- *I have the power to create new possibilities.*
- *Love begins with an appreciation of self.*
- *A new day brings new opportunities.*
- *God never withholds love.*

PRAYER

I know I will always love, in part, my beloved.
However, spiritually I embrace the creativity
that exists within me, and I joyously
move on to new adventures.

Did we mean what we said?
If not, do we mean what we are saying now?

Life is alive! Just as our bodies grow, and we embrace change on a daily basis, so it is with relationships.

In healthy relationships, individuals grow together, willingly accepting the changes that take place in their partners and seeking to work with the ever-new situations that arise. Nothing really stays the *same* for long!

This is also true for language. What we said five years ago, or twenty years ago, will evolve. The meaning and intent will change. Sometimes it does not look the same and what we said years ago we cannot (honestly) say today. Our feelings, understanding, insights, journey — everything has changed.

This has a direct connection with people who separate. They came together believing love alone would keep them bonded as a couple, only to realize their love has changed.

Even if the feelings of love are still there, the journey, passion, and needs have changed.

Lyrics (paraphrased) from *South Pacific* come to mind:

Who can explain? Who can tell you why?

Fools give their reasons. The wise never try!

Did we mean what we said? Yes. We did *then*. But things have changed. For some, there is a real need to separate. What worked then is not working anymore. This does not mean what was said in the past was a lie or fabrication, but things *do* change. *And nobody should be held to words spoken when things were different.*

Do we mean what we are saying now? Yes. If two people can grow together, give each other space, act honorably with integrity, and keep *reasonable* commitments, then the love partnership will remain and flourish. But nobody can really know, *really know*, if what they say and feel today they will inevitably feel years from now. It's true, some choose to remain in the "bed they made," and may God bless them. However, others, not easily or irresponsibly, make the choice to separate. And may God bless them, too!

Remember, we are talking separation, not divorce. Maybe they can return to the spiritual center of their words and renew their commitment, having learned important insights about themselves and their partner *through the separation*. Nobody should be nailed to the expressions they use!

PRAYER

God, today I am able to forgive myself for the promises I could not keep, knowing You understand the true hearts, desires, and limitations of our expressions.

You can walk away, but how do you forget?

You do not forget the people you love.

The connection made through love does not die. It may fade, but it does not die.

What needs to be remembered is *why* we walked away. Love is often painful, but it should not continually be a painful experience. Love is not always easy, but it should not be difficult on a daily basis. Love makes demands, but it should not cost you your sanity.

Sometimes we must love somebody enough to let them go.

Often we walk away so we can love again. A part of us knows if we stay in the unhealthy love relationship we will emotionally die, become depressed, hurt the children, so we need to let go.

There is a destructive kind of love, an unhealthy infatuation, a smothering obsession that destroys all who are involved in it. Sanity demands we walk away.

But you don't forget. It was not all bad. The good months or years were wonderful, the romance glorious, the feelings experienced were intense—it was not *all* bad. Maybe a part of you will be forever glad you had the experience and you know you have grown because of it. Still, you needed to walk away.

The wisdom of letting go should not really talk about mistakes; rather, it should affirm each love experience, even a painful one, is an opportunity to grow and learn.

We probably would do it all again, and change very little. Knowing, still, that the time would come for us to walk away.

PRAYER

Great Spirit, I'm so appreciative of the variety
of love experiences in my life and I thank You,
today, for the love that has left scars.
I honor my love wounds.

Today I'm learning to connect with where I am.

Separation gives us an opportunity to connect with where we are. Sometimes we simply need to be on our own. We need to find our own space, live in it, build walls to protect it, and honor it.

Why? Because maybe our life has been programmed to meeting other people's needs, making them happy, protecting them, and *giving, giving, giving*. We need to let go of a codependent lifestyle that is draining us, so we create *separation*.

We physically set ourselves apart in order to discover who we are, what our needs are, where we want to go in our lives, and what we believe in, and to find the path that will take us to *our bliss*.

We may need to separate from husband, wife, children, mother, father, or lover in order to find. Many will accuse us of selfishness, thoughtlessness, or irresponsibility, but we need to create a time, space, and place to connect with who we are. We've lived our whole life trying to make people happy — so, now we upset some people!

Sometimes the separation takes on a more mystical form. We create times of meditation, contemplation, and quiet, a space where we are alone and can slow down. Rest. Take time for ourselves. Feel our feelings.

"Be still and know that I am God."

Be still and know — who the hell are we? We deliberately *separate* ourselves from family and friends, create our space, and nobody should interrupt or trespass. We separate to create mental boundaries so we can grow spiritually. We are seeking ourselves, and eventually everyone will benefit.

PRAYER

I separate to involve myself in my life.
I close the door on life in order to be free.

I wish the Church would acknowledge my separation
because, God, how I need God in my life, now!

It has always seemed strange to me that the Church is involved in the celebration of marriage, yet is strangely absent during times of divorce and separation. Surely people need the presence of God, the comfort of the Church, and the inspiration the Holy Spirit can bring not just when things are going well, but when "we walk through the valley of the shadow."

It is those painful moments, when we just don't think we can go on, that the comfort of the Church is needed. Yet it is strangely absent!

Fortunately, there are exceptions. Some priests and ministers, and many metaphysical churches, have created "services" to acknowledge the spiritual journey into a divorce, or affirm the need for a separation, but generally speaking, people feel abandoned by the Church when they are separated or going through a divorce. It is words of comfort they need to hear. It is the feeling God has not deserted them they need to be in touch with.

Further, it is hearing, from a priest or minister, in the company of family and friends, that they are not bad people. The Church is present at the marriage. God is involved in the blessing of the relationship. Why, then, should people be left alone when things are not going well?

With this in mind, I wrote the following prayer:

"We came together to embrace the healing presence of the Holy Spirit for [_____], knowing God's loving presence surrounds us now, as God was present when the marriage was first celebrated. We know a separation is not easy. We acknowledge the pain of a relationship that for many reasons is not working out. We are not here to judge or blame. We are simply here to embrace God's love and seek the spiritual path for the future. We let go as we travel this painful path.

We know the journey of life is not always easy and sometimes people come together to celebrate and enjoy each other, then continue their journeys in different and separate directions. The memories remain. And they are not all negative. The love has changed, but can never be destroyed. Now is the time for appreciation. Forgiveness. The honest sharing of feelings. The wisdom of acknowledging we do not know the outcome. And it is okay. Amen."

I had to run away from the lover I feared.

Domestic violence is more widespread than many of us ever realized. Many therapists would say it is impossible to have fear in love, because the nature of love can never encompass fear. Love casts out fear. They are incompatible.

Yet the poet in me, while acknowledging the wisdom of the above, also knows nothing is completely black and white. Truth lives in the gray!

People sometimes love the people they fear. People stay, loving the abuser until the day they die. The complexity of love embraces those we fear, those we hate, and those we adore yet (sometimes) despise.

Few can understand this love.

- *It is sick.*
- *It is unhealthy.*
- *Everyone suffers, not least the children.*
- *It will always escalate to violence and more violence.*
- *Don't dignify this dysfunction in the same sentence as love.*

All true statements. Fortunately the person who made the opening statement decided to run away. The healing break has taken place and maybe she will begin to think about what she really wants to do with her future, explore loving from a distance and move into a new life, with new opportunities.

Can people finally break the sick cycle of fear that follows violent relationships like a deathly albatross? Yes, they can if they *really want to*.

Many have broken from a violent relationship, have *let go* because it was too, too painful. People can change, people do change, but people must *really want to change*.

That's the key. *What do you want to do?* I used to hear a professor say at the end of the day, people do what they want to do. Maybe. Maybe this person will run away only to return. Or maybe the fear is part of the love. The therapist in me says *no*, but the poet...

PRAYER

I accept just as there are many kinds of people,
with many kinds of needs, so there are many kinds of love.
For me, love is about healing, joy, serenity, and trust.
And I accept, although I do not endorse,
the love that includes fear.

Let go.

Two simple words that are breaking my heart.

It's not easy to let go. It's easy to say, but when it comes to the actual letting go, all the fears and insecurities arise. What are these fears all about? What are the insecurities?

We fear if we let go, there will be no one else, and we will be lonely. The mental picture arises of sitting in an empty house, in an empty room, with an empty fridge, and a telephone that never rings. If we have a dog, even our dog looks unhappy!

We fear if we let go, we will be walking away from something that could be great. Perhaps the relationship only needs a few more months, and it could be all we imagined. But if we walk away — nothing.

We fear our expectations may be too great. Everybody has bad days. Couples are not always communicating, making love, or laughing at the dinner table. We fear we are the problem. If we let go, all we will have is "the problem." Our insecurities connect to these fears. *We* are difficult, selfish, controlling, unreasonable, and the relationship did not work *because of us*!

If we are not careful, these fears and insecurities will lead us to pick up the phone (again) and return to the pain we want to let go. Now is the time to feel our pain. Find friends to talk with. Develop new interests, perhaps exercise, pick up the books we intended to read, go to a support group for codependency — do something!

These fears and insecurities are not based in reality. The relationship is not "not working" because of you. It takes two to tango, and two to create a dysfunctional relationship. Stop the blame; create a new game. You are not letting go because the problems have just arisen. It's taken a long time to reach the point of walking away. We need a new self-empowerment tape in our heads:

• *There are other people out there.*

• *It's not unreasonable to expect excitement and communication in a relationship.*

• *You are not the cause of all the problems.*

• *You may not be perfect, but you are special.*

• *Don't knowingly settle for second-best.*

Yes, it's painful to let go. But it was also painful, very painful, when you stayed. It's just that we so often forget the bad times and cling to the good times in our memories, and memories are not always factual.

PRAYER

God, I embrace my pain, loneliness, and fears.
I acknowledge my insecurities. But those are not who I am.
I am more.

*It was during my wedding service I realized
I did not love this person.*

Someone actually told me this after a conference on codependency I coordinated. Many other attendees identified.

Why was I surprised?

This was not the only shock. For over twenty years the woman whose story this is stayed in a loveless marriage, knowing from the very beginning she did not love her husband. Many others at the conference shared they had stayed for too many years in a loveless relationship, rather than separate.

Some of the reasons they gave:

- *Did not want to upset family plans.*
- *Hated to hurt the other person's feelings.*
- *There is more to life than having a happy marriage.*
- *Children stopped any chance of leaving.*
- *Where would I go? What would I do?*
- *She/he was very kind to me. I had everything, except love.*

The Wisdom of Letting Go

We must not forget how difficult it is to separate when you have made your vows to God, in the presence of a priest or minister, in the company of family and friends. The words, "Till death us do part," are taken literally by many people.

But does a God of love not want you to experience love? Also, would not this God of love forgive a person for marrying somebody they did not love? Not understand the reason for your separation? I think God would.

Separation is not only good for the person who does not love, it is also good for the *other* person. After separation, they have a chance to find a person who loves them and *wants* to be with them, rather than staying with somebody who *feels sorry for them*!

We deserve the best. known mediocrity is *not* the best.

Prayer

Today I am willing to risk upsetting people, even family,
so I can live my life with integrity.

I stayed for the children. But in the end,
even the children begged me to leave.

It really is not true if you have a Mom and Dad who stay together you always have a happy family. It really is not true the children do not know when Mom and Dad no longer love each other. It certainly and most definitely is not true violence in the family is less harmful than the family splitting up. Pain is pain; and in a family, everybody feels it.

We really do need to examine our religious rules that keep, either because of guilt or fear, or possibly both, married partners together in one house when love has exited through the window. We need to let go of religious rules that create pain and unhappiness. We need to let go of the thinking that tells us children do not understand, they never heard the arguments, and they were asleep when the serious drinking happened. We need to let go of the pretense of sacrifice, living our lives as victims for others, when it is really about *us*— our fear, confusion, and helplessness. We need to let go of a fantasy that wounds us and others, *and embrace a reality.*

In so many instances children have worked an intervention on their parents and convinced them to separate because it was just too damned painful to remain silent. The child has become the parent; the parents have become the *sickly* children.

I have letters from parents who have repeated some of what their children told them:

• *How could we not know the unhappiness that existed between you and Dad? The atmosphere was chilling. No wonder we never wanted to stay in the house.*

• *The house was not that big. We heard every word. Don't forget you were both shouting. Most nights I cried myself to sleep.*

• *I wanted a Mom and Dad who were happy. We never had that. I could be happy with Dad. I could be happy with Mom. But when they were together I hated them.*

• *You told me God wanted you to stay with Daddy. I was asking God to take us away!*

And a child shall lead them!

PRAYER

Great Spirit, today I try not to guess what a person is feeling. I try not to assume I know their needs. I find courage in your energy, and I ask them.

My separated lover died today. Something in me also died.

Separation does not mean the love has died. Often we separate because we love.

When you have shared special moments with somebody, slept with them, made love, taken vacations, laughed on a train in a foreign land, argued and cried together, something in both of you connects. *Really connects.* And such a love never separates, never dies, and can never turn into something less than love.

If that person, after you separate, is going through an awkward and difficult time, you feel their pain. When they get sick, you want to be near them, even if it means traveling a long distance. And yes, when they die, something in you dies.

But the memories don't die. The special way they talked, how they looked in the morning, the way they drank soup, that sign of nervousness few recognized, the gradual journey into old age and death, these things can never die because they have become a part of us. And something in us dies when they die.

An energy has been removed from our existence. Something has gone. It is absent. It was here with us, and now is no more.

My separated lover died today. Something in me also died.

But that something does not stay dead. Eventually a resurrection follows. We grieve. We let go. We walk in the shadow for however long it takes, and then it comes back.

The face, the voice, the style, the gratitude in knowing such a person—the memories return, and we smile again.

PRAYER

Today I embrace death as part of life.
I don't always like it, or understand it.
But it's part of the familiar.
And I know it awaits me.

*I think I'm becoming "New Age" because the
other day I felt strangely familiar in a foreign place,
and I realized I'd been here before.*

Separation is not just about being apart from somebody you love. Sometimes separation is used to describe an out-of-body experience, or a déjà vu.

Today I am able to separate myself from some of the things I was told in Church, and I'm aware of feelings *of having been in a certain situation before*. I've had this conversation before; I've seen this town and church, and just down the street there is a little grocery shop on the corner. I've met people I felt I knew, yet we'd never been introduced.

Sometimes I get an urge to telephone a friend and yes, they need me or were thinking about me that day. Coincidence? I don't think so!

If I am able to *separate* myself from the immediacy of my world and reconnect with my past, my heritage, and the accumulated memory bank of my family; if I am able to allow my imagination, acknowledging its collective history, to soar into the future, then I believe I can be an *intuitive prophet, seer, and priest*. But I must be willing to separate, detach, and remove my thinking from the apparent smallness of who I am and embrace *the more*.

Spirituality is involved in the act of separation and that spark of the divine that exists in all of us, and comes from God, is not limited. Our soul is not limited to yesterday or the present because, in a real sense, it also lives in the future.

Sometimes I believe I have lived other lives. my mind and body have recorded other experiences. I've had adventures at other times and in other places.

We often think too small.

PRAYER

God of yesterday, today, and tomorrow,
why is it so hard for some people to believe
Your spiritual continuum is within us?

Separation is easy for those who have never loved.

I think it is true to say if you care about a person, feel an affection for somebody, and a problem or conflict arises, then it is not too difficult to separate.

You will miss them. You will think of them often. Perhaps call or write a letter. Maybe sometimes you will even recall them in your conversations, *but none of this is love!*

Love is really about a passionate connection. It involves our feelings, mind, body, and primal urges and exudes an energy that produces a glow, a certain spontaneity, *a high*. It is much, much more than like, care, or affection.

When we separate from this love, it is really difficult, heart-breaking, and impossible to explain, except to those who have experienced it. Only they understand.

It is greater than any addiction because it encompasses everything. To separate from somebody we love involves a kind of death. It is the hangover of all hangovers.

The Wisdom of Letting Go

We think, at the time of separation, the craving for "the other" will never leave us. Our heart is broken.

Anyone who says this intensity is easy to break does not know of what they speak. A friendship is difficult to detach from, and a love, is extremely hard, never easy.

PRAYER
God of the Word, Who took flesh and experienced feelings, I connect with Your love that experienced both joy and pain, knowing the confusion of letting go of those You loved.

Love is connection, never separation.

When you think you have said all you know about separation, you suddenly realize the opposite seems, at times, also to be true!

How can you separate, really, from those you love? Perhaps you can stop loving, take time to transition the love into some kind of regard. You start off loving, and it moves into an affection, a genuine respect, and a kind of liking.

On the other hand, there is a kind of love that never dies, or fades, or develops into respect or regard — it is always *love*.

• *A mother's love for her child.*

• *A brother's love for his sister, and vice versa.*

• *A school friend who was your first love and has a special place in your heart.*

• *The impossible love that never really had a chance to grow.*

• *The love that dare not speak its name.*

Love is connection, never separation.

I understand this love and I know it to be dangerous, illogical, impossible, and sometimes doomed; yet I know this love. I cannot deny it.

All my reading about and intellectual acceptance of codependency and the need for separation cannot remove from me the *knowing* of this kind of love others may describe as unhealthy. The love I can never separate myself from, for it lives in me.

PRAYER

God of the opposites, you breathe a diversity that can never be fully comprehended in one thought. Today I struggle with living the confusion of life.

Please let me go.
And I will let you go.
In love.

This is the ultimate celebration of separation because it starts and ends in love.

Sometimes things do not work out. We want them to work out; we want everything to be happy, joyous, and free but our differing personalities make it impossible. We entered into the relationship believing it would never end, and we had no thought of *separation*, yet that thought, over time, emerged. We did not intend to hurt. We didn't want to argue. Never did we intend the children to suffer. But it happened.

Then we entered into the sick dance. I left only to return. You said you would not call but you did. We each promised that much-needed space, some time alone — no more letters, *please*. But always we followed each other into the sacred space, sent the letters, and created havoc.

We tried having friends meet with us, to get family involved. We shared our darkest feelings at support groups, and read every possible book on how to create a healthy relationship, to no avail. We tried through our tears to make our love work.

We established boundaries. Prayed in church. Went on retreats separately and together. Even attempted vacations in exotic places, followed always by the tears, anger, and separation. We tried to make our love work.

And now we are tired. Exhausted. Too many wasted years. Too many opportunities lost. Life was slipping away from both of us. Enough.

Please let me go. And I will let you go. In love.

PRAYER

God, You never said life would be easy.
And I never thought it would be this difficult.
But I do not come to you complaining, only confused.

Divorce

Chapter 5

God, I never thought it would be over,
but it's over.

When you've loved somebody deeply for a number of years, then it ends, of course it is devastating. Maybe there is some relief, even joy, but there must also be the ingredients of pain, waste, and confusion.

People do not marry thinking about divorce. They marry with their minds full of hope, adventure, future plans, and family. Nobody marries thinking divorce.

Why does love end? There is no singular answer:

• *We grew apart over the years.*

• *I loved her, but it simply was not enough. I needed more. I grew and she remained the same.*

• *I loved what I did not know. The man I loved was soon replaced by an angry, violent person. I often wonder where the man I married went.*

• *When the children came he changed. He was jealous of the children. He wanted all the attention. Eventually he went out to get it.*

• *I never wanted the divorce. She came home and announced she had fallen in love with somebody else. I still love her.*

So many paths culminate in one word: divorce. Finished. Over. A new and different chapter begins.

Whatever the reasons, there is always the pain. I think it is important to acknowledge this pain and find help.

- *With close friends and family.*
- *A therapist.*
- *A support group.*
- *A journal or healing workbook.*

A divorce creates death in life: the death of dreams, the family unit as it was, the familiar, and the myriad qualities that made the other person special.

People will say:

- *Get over it.*
- *You're better off without him/her.*
- *You'll find somebody else.*

It is true you will get over it in time. You might be better off on your own, and maybe you will find somebody else. However, feel the pain. Cry the tears. Express your anger. Only then will you heal.

PRAYER

God, my sadness is in knowing it is finally over.
I bring You my sadness with no expectations
other than knowing You are present with me

So we said we would never part.
And now I'm divorced.

People say things and mean them at the time. But people change. And when they change, the feelings they once had also change.

Nobody stays the same.

Some people are able to live a commitment, and that is honorable. Others discover honor in owning their change of feelings. They speak and honor the death of love.

Beginning a conversation that will inevitably cause pain requires great courage:

• *What I am about to say is very hard for me, but it is not fair to either of us to continue the pretense. What I am about to say I know you know. We have grown apart.*

• *When I fell in love with you I thought it would never end. Never before or since have I known such a love. But the love I felt so strongly has died. I know what I am saying hurts you. I know it will hurt the children. But to continue, I believe, will cause more pain.*

• I never thought I could love anybody more than I loved you. However, since we have been separated, I have been dating somebody. And I am in love. I also feel guilty. We have been friends during the separation and I now feel I should begin a new chapter in my life. Hopefully we will remain friends.

There is no easy way to say we want a divorce. But if a marriage has ended, those words need to be said. Silence only adds to the confusion and soon drifts into deceit.

Better to pluck up the courage and express what you are feeling. Chances are the rehearsal you have been practicing in your head has been far more painful than the reality of the *actual* conversation.

PRAYER

Eternal Friend, when I heard the words I felt a quiet relief.
The waiting, the anticipation during our separation,
was far more horrendous than the reality
of our meeting over coffee.

Love is not always forever.
Why didn't anybody tell me?

When you were in love, it wouldn't have made much difference what people had said! In any case, who wants to start a marriage thinking it might not last? None of us is blind. We see every day that marriages end. People separate. Divorce is a reality.

Would we really want to stay in a marriage if the other person had ceased to love us and desperately wanted out? How can it be healthy to stay in a sacred union that has ceased to be sacred?

As painful as it might be to contemplate what life would be like divorced, it is surely more painful to be in bed with a partner who has become your *separated* friend — maybe not even a friend!

The picture so many of us grew up with:

- *White wedding.*
- *Picket fence cottage.*
- *Children playing in the garden.*
- *Joyously attending children's wedding with adoring in-laws.*
- *Grandchildren who visit every Sunday to eat apple pie.*

This tinsel picture of what our life should be like often adds to our feelings of failure and sadness. The truth is separation and divorce are a reality for many people and, while we don't want to give divorce any energy when we attend a wedding, we certainly don't want to blame ourselves if it crosses our path.

Nobody wants a divorce; but for many it is part of their spiritual journey.

Maybe there is value in being grateful for the happy times, the children who come from the marriage, and the grandchildren who carry on the characteristics and personalities of their forebears. These reminders help us to grow.

PRAYER

God, I'm learning so much about myself from this divorce.

My resentments have mellowed into a gentle acceptance.

I realize I am more than my marriage.

I am more than a spouse. I am more than a parent.

I am becoming my own person.

Why do I feel so sinful just because I'm divorced?
I was left. It wasn't my fault!

The sadness for me, as a clergyman, is in how the Church has punished many people because their marriage did not work out:

• *Divorce is a sin. You are divorced. Therefore you are a sinner.*

• *Had you walked with Jesus, this divorce would never have happened.*

• *A marriage is not blessed unless you attend the Church. Your marriage ended when you ceased to attend church.*

• *It is the sacraments that hold a marriage together.*

• *It takes two to make a marriage. It takes two to create a divorce. You are both guilty in the eyes of God.*

So many people feel sinful, guilty, weak, rejected, and *judged by the Church.* In reality, surely the opposite should be the case. The Church should be there for both partners and the family.

It should be offering Jesus' healing words of comfort. It should provide a sacred service of nurturing support for those who are being divorced and journeying on separate paths.

I suggest offering a prayer like the following:

Dear God,

We come together to honor the decision of [_____] and [_____] who have decided to divorce after a life of celebrated marriage.

We know it is not easy for either of them, and we do not meet here in Your loving presence to judge or condemn; rather are we here to acknowledge their decision in Your presence.

We commit ourselves to a continued friendship and nurturing support (for them and the children) knowing Your presence is as real to them in their divorce as it was in their marriage.

We bless and honor them as they begin their separate paths, trusting Your love will be reflected in their lives and future relationships.

Amen.

I never knew we were together <u>and</u> separate.

Words are beautifully strange, and at times a phrase that appears so loving and nurturing can later create guilt and confusion.

• *You are joined together as husband and wife.*

• *What God has joined together let no one separate.*

People read and hear these words and think their *individual* identity has been sacrificed in marriage, their individual personalities and characters fused into a single identity.

This is not really true. Kahlil Gibran articulated a higher idea when he wrote, "Let there be space in your togetherness."

Marriage is a partnership, a working together of two people, with shared joys and responsibilities, but *enmeshment* is never a characteristic of a healthy marriage.

Divorce affirms our distinctiveness. What grew together can sometimes grow apart. In light of Gibran's view, in divorce the space gets exaggerated at the cost of togetherness!

Sad. Tragic. Painful. But a fact for many couples. Nobody would want a divorce in an "ideal" world because it reflects part of human *imperfection* and *brokenness*.

In the real world, there are not only bad things, but also sad things. Divorce is sad.

However, because we are separate, not fused together, when the divorce happens, we will survive. It's not true that half of ourselves walked out of the door leaving us helpless.

We will survive. Possibly remarry. Certainly we will be happier than living in a loveless marriage.

PRAYER

Great Spirit, today I am aware of my special,
distinct personality.
I rejoice in my divine individuality.
In this awareness is my survival.

I'm divorced, but I'm still connected.

Throughout this book, although we're dealing with many aspects of letting go, there is a spiritual theme that seems to hold everything together—connection.

Love is a strangely divine energy that, once experienced, never seems to *die*. We say divorce is the death of a marriage but it is not the death of love.

Many divorced people speak of a love that surprisingly endures:

• I've not seen him for years, yet sometimes I hear a phrase on the TV, or smell the cologne he used to wear, or see the back of a man walking with a certain gait, and I remember him. Funny, but I suppose I still love him.

• When I heard she passed away, although we had not spoken or seen each other for over twenty years, something in me died. Yet something in me still lives – my love for her.

• He was not a good man. Certainly he proved to be a terrible husband. I'm glad I divorced him. My present husband is wonderful. But you know, I still think about him. A part of me still loves him. It's the darndest thing. Crazy, really.

Love is a feeling that rarely dies. For most of us who have been touched by love, it lingers. This is *connection*.

Divorce is a crossroads, a change in direction, and a letting go of the past, but it's not the death of the past!

Even the painful needs to be remembered. We will never return, yet it is forever a part of us.

PRAYER

The love connection helps affirm my faith in You.
Even my divorce, the end of my marriage,
involves and includes You.
The love I feel today, even for those who hurt me,
manifests my connection with You.

I married for better or for worse.
That should have been a warning.

It's hard to talk about divorce without talking about marriage. The Church hesitantly prepares us in the text, "for better or for worse," for the fact that some marriages are not good, happy, joyous, or loving. Maybe they start out that way. Maybe in the very early stages they showed promise, but some marriages were not "made in heaven." The love and affection faded, things got worse, and eventually it became awful — then divorce.

Many people who have experienced divorce saw it coming:

• *You know, it's a funny thing to say, and I'm a little ashamed, but when I was walking down the aisle in my beautiful white gown, I had a sense of dread. I "kinda liked" him, but I did not think the marriage was a good idea. However, my father liked him. My mother felt he would be able to take care of me. Also, the invitations had been sent out and the meal had been paid for in advance! But I confess, I did have that feeling as I walked down the aisle.*

• *The wedding night was a disaster. I knew it was only a matter of time. We both understood that night we would not be having children!*

• He always had an eye for the ladies. I even noticed him looking at the wedding reception. The marriage went downhill from the beginning. He loved me, I'm sure. But he loved others as well. He felt trapped in the marriage; and I suffocated.

If only we trusted our intuition. If only we spent more time developing our spiritual instincts.

Divorce is a reminder that life delivers consequences.

PRAYER

*I know today to trust my inner feelings
and act upon them.
I let go of my feelings of insecurity and fear,
embracing the spiritual power
that protects my wellbeing.*

Marriage is about love, not contract.

I'm outside the courtroom with a piece of paper in my hand that tells me the last sixteen years are over — divorce. How can a marriage be reduced to a piece of paper?

In actuality, it cannot. I remember the Jesuits telling me the only time you knew a marriage was true and blessed by God, is when that marriage lasted until death! If it ends in divorce then it was never *essentially* a Christian marriage. That was Jesuit logic in the sixties. I'm not sure what they would say today.

There is a spiritual perspective that says not all marriages are meant to last. People come together, share with each other, take what they need, and then a point in time arrives when they journey separately but remain *connected*. We let go of the anger, frustration, and disagreements. We bless each other, then move on.

Some people would subscribe today to the idea that marriage is a contract, a social agreement, or a business relationship that involves love, but is not solely about love. There is more to marriage than *love*.

I expect the truth is mingled in all the above, but there is a *mystery* about marriage that can never be fully explained or understood. It certainly cannot be delineated in a written agreement.

A divorce symbolizes one or both partners need to separate and move on. Pain is usually involved. One thing is for sure, life goes on. Our attitude about divorce can make all the difference in how we survive it.

• *Some move on and make a new life with a new partner.*

• *Some remain angry and resentful until death.*

• *Some put their lives on hold and wait for their partner to return. Risky business.*

• *Others die in life.*

Whatever marriage is, a piece of paper that says it happened cannot explain it. And neither can the paper that says it ended!

PRAYER

God, in Your presence I burn the paper
that tells me I'm divorced.
I no longer am focused on what used to be.
Today I embrace the freedom that comes with tomorrow.

This time it's over.

There are many endings before the end:

• *I'm sick of this life; nothing seems to be working in this marriage.*

• *You seem so cold. Distant. Aloof. I don't know how to get close to you anymore.*

• *Get out. Take your clothes. Take what you need and don't come back.*

• *Last night the children came into the bedroom and asked what was wrong. It's beginning to affect them.*

• *Your mother called and asked where you were. I couldn't make up another lie. I told her I did not know.*

Then the scary point is reached when you know, *really know*, it's over.

I'm leaving. Don't try to call me. I'll get in touch later through my attorney.

Please do what I ask. We both know it's for the best.

The person means what they are saying.

Divorce is always preceded by the awful moment of knowing there is nothing more to be done, and nothing more to be said, for nothing works anymore. There is only pain.

What is important is to feel the pain. Let go of the blame. Let go of the compromise. Let go of all the excuses. These are the dynamics that have brought us to this point.

Now we let go, and embrace God.

PRAYER

Lord, sometimes I catch myself thinking there
is one last chance left, but it's over.
Continue to hold me in Your love.

Today I know I will be alone.
But tomorrow is another day.

I suppose in order to survive a divorce we must be optimistic. We know every divorce has its pain, and at the time we feel the pain will never end.

But for most people it does end:

• *People told me it would get better. I didn't believe them. But I'm happier today than I've been anytime in my life. And it's only been ten months since the divorce was final.*

• *My divorce nearly killed me. I drank. Took pills. Saw a therapist for nine months, hoping that would get us back together. Then, I can't really explain it, I woke up one morning and said out loud, "This is ridiculous!" From that moment my life started to change. I'm still alone but I'm happy.*

• *My children helped me get over it. I saw them pick up their lives, dry their tears, and move on. I admired them so much. They became my teachers.*

As a clergyman, I've often been involved in helping people get over their divorce pain. Most find it helpful, in the early stages, to talk. They talk the pain out.

But others need to ritualize the death of their marriage:

• *Burn the pictures, letters, and communal furniture.*
• *Place the wedding ring in a casket box and bury it.*
• *Sell the house and move to a new area.*

The new day that follows a divorce calls for a new attitude. Nobody else can do that for us.

CHIN UP. DEEP BREATH. OUT YOU GO.

PRAYER

God, it's a strange thing to say in my prayers,
but tomorrow I'm going to get my hair cut,
ask for a different style, and a new color.
Then I'm going shopping.
Thought You'd like to know. Amen.

When I divorced I died;
nobody told me there was life after marriage.

The messages we receive while growing up frequently indicate the purpose of life is to get married, have children, then prepare for the grandkids:

• *You will grow up and find a nice young man/woman.*

• *Why aren't you married?*

• *It's time you were settled, with a spouse, starting a family.*

• *God said it is not good to be alone, hence the instituted sacrament of marriage.*

• *We have only half an existence until we meet the person of our dreams.*

The reinforcement and culmination of all such messages often drives a person into an early marriage and then, when it ends in divorce — *nothingness*. You are less than a whole person. If you suffered the guilt created by religious abuse, you also consider yourself a sinner. After divorce, only death!

We will only change this situation when we are able to let go of the unhealthy messages that suggest marriage is the only *true* focus in life.

• *Some marriages do not work out, and it is very possible we can live positive and healthier lives single.*

• *We should appreciate the marriage for what it was; we move on knowing other, healthier, relationships await us.*

• *God's loving presence is ever available to heal our brokenness. If the marriage ended in divorce, then the worst is probably over!*

As we live in the new millennium, we do not need to buy into other peoples' understanding of happiness, especially when we know we were not happy. Better to move on and create a life that fits our needs and attitudes.

PRAYER
*God, I'm understanding people put too
many words in Your mouth.
I'm seeking, today, to hear Your loving voice.*

When half your life dies, you die.

I remember my mother saying you don't have a full, whole life as a single person. Marriage was the only relationship to focus on.

Growing up I heard many members of my family feeling *sorry* for aunts and other relatives who found themselves single.

It's so sad about Mary. I really don't know what's wrong with her, but she is still single, living in that house alone. Yet she loves children. I wish she would get married again. It's not natural. Of course she pretends to be happy. She never complains. Always with a smile on her face. Off making friends in all those foreign countries. More money than sense, if you ask me. Selfish really. But nobody will ever tell me it's natural for a young, healthy girl to be traveling all over the world having fun, or so she says, with no husband. I don't know who she takes after!"

The truth is, each of us is a *whole person* unto ourselves. We certainly don't need a spouse or children to make us whole. Indeed, we don't *all* need husband, wife, children, or grandchildren to be fulfilled. God has made us complete.

That being said, we need friendships, relationships outside of ourselves, and a life that is not only about our needs. However, we don't *need* to take people home with us.

I know many single people who are extremely happy and fulfilled. I know many married couples who are tragically sad. Hobson's choice.

Much better to concentrate our energy on finding out what makes us happy and let other people get on with their lives. Making people feel *less than* because they don't live as we do is surely pathetic.

PRAYER

I let go of all expectations concerning other people, and focus on living my life in a positive and creative manner.

It has taken me years to understand our divorce
was not about me, but about us.

Absolutely. It takes two to tango, and it takes two to stop the dance.

We really need to let go of all the guilt and shame concerning divorce because it keeps us stuck in yesterday.

• *I did something wrong.*

• *If only I'd tried more when the kids came along.*

• *I should have complained less and endured more. My mother was right!*

• *I was not a faithful wife. After all, the husband is the head of the household. I am told by my Church to be submissive. I should have kept my mouth shut.*

These tapes must be erased. They feed codependency, low self-esteem, and shame. *These tapes keep saying you are a bad person.* Erase them!

Replace them with affirmations that tell you:

• *I am special, and loved by God.*

• *I do not need anyone else to make me complete.*

- *I no longer will live with abuse and put-downs.*

- *I need to find a spiritual teacher who will interpret the scriptures in a spiritual light, emphasizing positiveness and self-esteem.*

- *I loved my spouse. But I also need to love me. This is my focus today.*

It's very hard at first to understand, especially for those of us who were brought up in the fifties and sixties, that we are not responsible for how other people feel or act.

We *alone* are not responsible for a divorce.

<u>*PRAYER*</u>

God of Health and Wellness,
I will no longer wallow in guilt and shame.
Today I affirm my freedom
and let go of all my yesterdays.

Love is not forever.

This is something of an overstatement. Because we have experienced a divorce we must guard against applying our situation to everyone. Some people are very happy in their marriages and love until death.

My mother and father are a good example of this. They have been married for over sixty years and truly have enjoyed a delightful and loving marriage. Of course they've had their ups and downs. Arguments. Fights. Occasional walk-outs. But the hard times have been few compared to the good times.

Their *love connection* has lasted, matured, and grown. At the time of writing my parents are still alive, living in England, and both are in their eighty-seventh year.

Here are a few remembrances I have of their views on marriage and divorce:

• *Mother: When I first met your father I thought he was a silly little man. But his silliness grew on me. He persisted in calling on me and asking me out (my mother despised him, initially, because he was a Catholic). One day I knew he was the man for me. Sixty years later, I still believe that.*

• Dad: Some of our friends got divorced. They grew apart. Their love died, I suppose. I've never stopped loving Maud. I'm eighty-seven and I still love her. Recently I was in the hospital for six days and I couldn't wait to get home to be with her. I suppose we're fortunate. I know my love is forever.

For some people the above is not true. Not good or bad, just different.

What is important to stress is not marriage or divorce, but the quality of our lives, the spiritual health of our relationships. Staying together should never be the goal; it's the quality of the time together.

PRAYER

Love is forever. Love is not forever.
Both are true in human life.
But Your love is everlasting.

I do not own my wife. She wants a divorce,
and I don't want to fight her anymore.
I do not need to die for love.

Sometimes it's very hard to go along with a divorce when *you* still love, *you* still want to try, or *you* think resolution is possible. But we do not *own* the feelings of another, not even those of our spouse!

Even when both partners feel a divorce is necessary, still there is pain. Once the decision has been made to split, separate, go on separate paths, better to let go of the control.

• *I love you enough to let you go. And I bless you on your path.*

• *I respect the differences we both have; I also respect the years we have spent together.*

• *I cannot make you love me. You cannot stop me loving you. But I know life will go on after both of us. How we respond to what is happening can make a big difference in how we feel about future relationships. I choose to respond in love.*

• *I am a romantic, but I do not want to die in this marriage. I will work on the wisdom of letting you go.*

In so many areas of life we are learning we do not own another person. Indeed, we do not own our own lives.

Our life is not dependent upon *our* permission; we grow old in spite of ourselves!

What about suicide? I don't believe that is the end. All we have accomplished with suicide is to force our existence along a notch and push ourselves into the next level. I do not know the consequences of such an act, and neither do you!

PRAYER

God, I'm learning to let go of the ownership,
control, and feeling of responsibility that
consumed my life for so many years.
I'm finding things are very much the same,
only I feel better.

I'm here. You are elsewhere.

Divorce. Thank God.

At last I have a chance to find happiness.

Oscar Wilde declared, "Marriage is a wonderful institution. But who wants to live in an institution?"

Funny. But true for many people.

Some marriages are awful and the only sane response is divorce:

• Every night I feared him coming through the door. Was the dinner ready. Were the kids behaving. Did the house look clean. God, for twenty years I lived with emotional pain. Then a friend said two words that changed my life: "Get out."

• My spouse was not abusive but the marriage was. I suffocated in an existence — I wouldn't call it living — because I was raised to believe divorce is a sin. Then I found a happy church where many of the congregants are divorced — hope.

• From the day I got married I was made to feel inadequate. I felt I was at school, with a teacher, and school never ended. Thank God we didn't have children. When I signed the divorce papers, I cried for joy. Today I feel free.

The Wisdom of Letting Go

There are so many people who learn their divorce was *so right*. And God still loved them.

The world did not come to an end.

Marriage is a loving relationship in which each partner is free to grow in love and gentle caring. It is not an institution.

PRAYER

My divorce was the best thing that happened to me.
I'm enjoying life for the first time.
God, divorce is Your blessing.

God knows I tried. God knows s/he tried.
Now, perhaps, we can both find love.

The purpose of a marriage is not to be in a *permanent* state of *trying*. No marriage should be that hard.

Sometimes people find instead of marriage they have a friendship. Friendship is good, but it is not marriage.

As we have already discovered in this book, it is very hard to describe or explain *love* because it takes different forms, with different expectations. It usually involves the physical, mental, and emotional connection, but then there is a certain "X" factor that cannot be explained, that *spark* only those involved feel.

• *Often it is not sensible.*

• *Rarely is it convenient.*

• *Always it is mysterious.*

However, it is different from friendship. Perhaps we can describe it as *the next stage*, the elusive point beyond what friends normally would have; it is love.

The act of trying is sometimes involved when the marriage is going through a rocky stage, but the *process* of love is not about trying!

When something is hard on a consistent basis, then usually something is wrong. The above statement suggests the two people are trying to make something work, trying to make it into something it is not.

Love should not be that difficult.

PRAYER

God, I realize Your love is not an effort.
It freely flows from who You are.
his is the love I seek to discover
in the living of my life.

Love is big enough to include divorce.

Just because you divorce a person does not mean you do not love them. It is the marriage that *did not work*. Love may still be alive and kicking!

• *I love him but I cannot live with him.*

• *The love changed once we got married. Now we are divorced, and things are like they used to be.*

• *She simply was not the marrying kind. She always hated institutions!*

Marriage is more than a commitment. It is a partnership that creates a *team relationship*, working together on home, finances, and family issues. It's not enough to say you love a person; you need to also *work together*.

Some people cannot or will not do this. They are so *individual* in their attitudes and outlook that the concept of partnership is an anathema to them!

Divorce, or a separated marriage, is inevitable for such people.

Of course there are some people who get married while intending to continue the single lifestyle. You might love them, but it's hard to be the only person rowing in the boat!

Better to get out and find somebody who is willing to be a partner in life. Or remain single. In the long run you will have less stress than trying to *force* a marriage relationship.

Remember, divorce is sad, not bad! You are not a sinful person because things did not work out. Nobody can predict how the future will be, especially when it involves people other than yourself.

PRAYER

God, I no longer beat myself up because I'm divorced.
Stuff happens.
I'm affirming a positive relationship with myself
and I'm open to the call of love.

Please know I love you.
I will always love you.
We just shouldn't be married.

Sometimes you know something about yourself that needs to be acted upon, and acted upon fast. We all change. And our changes affect other people.

Maybe we need to say something the other person is not going to like. Maybe they will get upset, angry, or hurt.

Our codependency kicks in and we stuff what we needed to say! Not a good idea.

Why? Because we enter into a sick cycle, knowing what we *need* to say will rise to the surface again, only to be stuffed.

Some people continue this behavior for years:

• *I know the marriage is dead. And I'm pretty sure s/he knows. But I don't have the courage to talk about it.*

• *She is such a good woman. I don't want to hurt her.*

• *I keep praying for a miracle. But our bed is the loneliest place on the planet!*

• *I think we both stayed for the children. Not a good idea. They seem more unhappy than we are.*

• *I keep saying I love him. He keeps saying he loves me. But our home is not a loving place.*

Really, it's harder to stay than it is to pluck up the courage and speak what we are feeling.

• *Maybe this book will help.*

• *Maybe we need to see a therapist.*

• *Maybe we need to begin the conversation with, "What I'm about to say is really hard for me. It's about our marriage… Please know I love you. I will always love you. We just shouldn't be married."*

PRAYER

Dear Spirit of Truth, for too long I said,
"I can't share my feelings."
Today I've been guided to write my feelings down.
Then I sit and read them to those involved.
And it's working. I'm feeling free.

*Spirituality brings the acceptance of
divorce to my life.*

Tough things happen in life. Not every day is a great day. Sometimes life hurts.

My divorce hurt me:

• *I felt used.*

• *I felt the marriage had been a sham. A waste of time.*

• *I felt our divorce had hurt and abused the children.*

• *I felt a failure.*

• *I wanted to kill the other man. And kill her. Then I felt guilty.*

• *I hadn't done anything wrong. If there was any justice in this world he would be suffering, and so would she.*

So much for an ever-loving God!

Then a friend shared it was not just about me. Although the divorce was personal, it was not a divinely organized tragedy.

Sad things happen in life. I needed to *let go,* or forever live the life of a whining victim.

The friend who spoke with me, gently, was a recovering alcoholic who shared about spiritual awakening, and how we need to *accept reality* rather than live a life of *appearances*. It made sense.

I wrote about my fear. My anger. My disintegrating expectations.

Over time I experienced acceptance.

PRAYER

Today I'm learning to let go of the need
to control and direct life.
Needless to say, I'm less stressed.
And I'm noticing the beauty that is hidden in life.

Sexism

Chapter 6

I do not believe a woman is a rib.
Therefore, I should not treat her that way.

Historically, I believe women have suffered from religious abuse more than any other single group, although gays and lesbians, people of color, and the physically disabled have also been discriminated against.

The scriptural text in Genesis that suggests God made Eve from the rib of Adam gave vent to the following specious arguments:

- *Women are secondary to men, and dependent.*
- *Their role is to be a "helper" to the male.*
- *Women should be submissive to the male.*
- *Women should make men happy and fulfil their every need.*
- *It is the duty of a wife to obey her husband.*

I am not a fundamentalist. I do not believe God made woman from a rib. I find the discussion silly. More than silly, it is abusive.

We should cease to interpret scriptural texts in a literal fashion because the damaged caused is considerable.

The Wisdom of Letting Go

Why is it so offensive to interpret the scriptures?

• *When Jesus refers to Peter as a rock, nobody takes that literally. The concept of the papacy was developed from the interpretation of this text.*

• *When Paul suggests slaves be obedient to their masters, this is not an argument for slavery.*

The deliberate selection of texts, especially those concerning women and homosexuals, only suggests an ulterior motive of *some preachers*.

Women are equal to—yet different from—men. Where they have the ability and strength, women should be allowed to pursue any goal or profession that is open to men, including priesthood.

Alleluia!

PRAYER

God, I know You created women with equal
partnership in the co-creative challenge,
and I thank You. Amen.

Today I am willing to let go of the religious
teachings that have created abuse.

In the name of God people have been abused.

So much sexism is based upon ignorant and prejudicial religious thinking that is passed on from one generation to another:

• *Women were created to please men.*

• *Jesus called men to the priesthood, therefore only men can be priests. (Did Jesus call any Chinese people to the priesthood? I've met many Chinese priests!)*

• *God created Adam and Eve, not Adam and Steve.*

• *The woman is not the head of the household. She should concentrate on being godly and submissive.*

The joy of living the spiritual life is experienced in the openness and sense of involvement taking place *globally*. The Christian is learning from the Hindu; the Muslim shares poetry with the Jew; the Buddhist seeks to listen and respect everyone.

Sexism has no place in the religion of the New Millennium. It is abhorrent, and as dated as the

Crusades, slavery, and homophobia. It misses completely the spiritual radiance and healing power of the feminine mystique. Sexism obliterates God.

PRAYER

Divine Spirit, sometimes I know I have let go of so much. "What is left?" I ask myself.

"The gold," You reply.

A sexist male is in search of his penis!

This is such a strong statement, but I believe a person who is prejudiced and seeks to make other people feel "less than" is insecure.

A man who is secure in himself is able to live with people who are different. He will treat a woman with respect and dignity, knowing she has gifts and talents he does not have. In so doing he will be able to give and receive, discovering the ebb and flow of spirituality. If your ego is dependent upon statements and attitudes that make others inferior, then something is seriously wrong with you.

I remember reading a letter from a woman who said her husband would scream and shout at her if she did something wrong. If the meal was not ready on time, or there was dust on the furniture, he would slap her until she cried for mercy. This made him feel superior, and he wanted her to beg.

He was also a "fundamentalist type" Christian, often quoting the scriptures that made reference to women remaining *submissive* to their husbands. Although they lived in a small apartment, he would expect her to treat him like a king, slippers ready when he returned from work. Every night he would find fault with something, often muttering phrases like, "This is what I should expect from a *mere* woman."

He was angry. Violent. His religion did not make him a happy man, and he seemed determined to make his wife unhappy with him. *And he was impotent.*

He was really unhappy with himself. He felt insecure because of his sexual dysfunction. He was "in search of his penis!"

I believe a sexist person is basically insecure, and it is most important for others not to buy into the game. Better to let go of all the nonsense, get help or therapy as a couple and, if that does not work, walk away with dignity.

PRAYER

Great Healer, I am aware people often project their sickness onto others. Today I will not enable this sick behavior, and I establish healthy boundaries.

An intolerant and abusive woman is no less dangerous than an intolerant and abusive man.

When we hear the word "sexist" we usually think of a male, and perhaps most sexists are. But occasionally you hear statements from a woman that indicate sexism is truly catholic — coming in all shapes and sizes:

• *Men are interested in only one thing. They have a penis brain.*

• *A child needs a mother. The father is less important.*

• *Men are not built to be sensitive; they are incapable of feeling.*

• *God practiced on man, and got it right when He created woman!*

We all need to let go of stereotypes that suggest *all men* do this or *all women* are like that. Sexism is abusive as it fails to recognize the spiritual qualities that exist in both sexes. A woman who discriminates against and puts down males is no less dangerous than a male who wants women to be submissive. Both are insecure.

PRAYER

God, I know some people in my life have abused me. Today I seek to recognize Your dignity in all creation.

Masculinity is stronger when it embraces femininity.

I always say if you really want to know me, you must embrace the *more.* I'm *more* than English, *more* than recovering, *more* than white, and *more* than male!

Sexism works on a black and white principle — division. It suggests male and female are separate, the male superior. It is not true to suggest the male, simply because he is male, is superior to the female. It is also not true their *separateness* is so very distinct.

I'm very aware of the feminine aspects of my nature, and feel stronger because of them. I've also met many women who are in touch with their "masculine" side, and they feel the stronger for it.

We must let go of stereotypes that keep people in neat little boxes, all wrapped up and distinct. The spiritual path affirms our *inclusiveness*, which necessarily entails our *genderedness.*

PRAYER

You are to be discovered in the gray areas of life. You have created us in variety, manifest in every human being.

Today I refuse to place women in a box
built and secured by men.

Sometimes when I hear certain male friends talking about women, their words seem to imply "thing-ness," or women as objects.

• *I like the way some of them look, especially after they've made themselves presentable with makeup.*

• *I'm glad they have more opportunities today, but I hope they don't get too cocky.*

• *I never knew what they had to complain about. We supported them. All they needed to do was keep the house clean and take care of the children.*

• *I don't like it when women talk about sex, and what their needs are. It makes them cheap. A good woman should be above all of that.*

• *She has a great pair of boobs. A wonderful figure. If I were not married, I'd want some of that.*

• *I went to the company meeting about increasing sales. The chairperson was a great looking broad. Why do they pick such cuties to run meetings? I couldn't keep my eyes off her figure. I kept imagining her naked in bed.*

Women are not for men's amusement. They are not sex objects. They are more than beauty. The old macho approach that is so abusive to both women and men needs to go. Women are coming out of the box created by men.

Sexism turns on the principle that men are superior to women, and much of what is acceptable and reasonable for men is denied women. Sexism makes the relationship between men and women "non-equal," disproportionate, and irrational. It is also abusive to men because as long as we treat women as objects, we miss a powerful spiritual energy on the planet only a woman can bring.

PRAYER
God, You must surely weep at the way
Your children treat each other.
But many of us, both men and women,
are rising up dry Your tears.

The principle of letting go involves my attitude
toward the opposite sex.

I think most of us would agree our emotional environment growing up, and the conditioning we underwent in society, has contributed to our attitudes and feelings about so many things:

• *How we treat people of ethnicities other than our own.*

• *The manner in which we seek to discuss and understand homosexuality.*

• *What we experience at a sacred site that is different from our personal religion.*

• *Our attitudes toward foreigners.*

• *The way we relate to and talk with women.*

This book addresses all the above issues, but it is the last item that concerns this chapter. It is undeniably true that women have been discriminated against for centuries. Even the Genesis writer implies God created Eve to meet the needs of man! On a recent TV documentary concerning the plight of women in Pakistan, it was shown that many, and I mean many, women are physically abused by their husbands, some *set afire with gasoline.* Few if any charges are ever brought against the men involved. The abuses in Pakistan, and in many other countries throughout the world, revolve around stripping women of legal and religious rights that enable them to confront their male abusers.

Here is the gist of what some of the women in Pakistan said:

• *I cannot confront my husband, or he will throw me out of the house. My family will not support me. What can I do?*

• *My husband treats me the same way my father treated my mother. She is now dead, thank God. My fear is for my children — they are both girls.*

• *The second time he set me on fire I called the police. They asked me what I had done. My family came to the hospital to criticize my stubborn behavior they believed provoked the burning.*

How can we realistically deal with codependency, sexual abuse, and dysfunctional families until we rid ourselves of the poison of sexism that is *blocking* the spiritual dialogue.

PRAYER
God, I know there is injustice throughout the world,
and I'm praying for a healing of the planet.
However, today I am also seeking
to give my prayers feet.

When I am able to get in touch with my feminine side,
my masculinity is strengthened.

In a conversation after a workshop I presented on "Spirituality and the New Millennium," I shared with several women a funny *true* story about me and flying:

When I travel, I'm often asked the question, "What do you do?" I always respond with, "Guess!" Invariably the answer is, "Are you a hairdresser? Or a clothing designer?"

The women laughed heartily, and so did I .

Then one of the women said something I will never forget: "The people on the airplane pick up on your creative *sensitivity*. Your feminine energy. Your *softness* is like that often observed in hairdressers and designers. It is a beautiful gift, Fr. Leo."

I believe this to be so true for me, and I have also witnessed the same from others, both men and women. When we are able to embrace for ourselves *the energy of the opposite sex,* we are personally stronger.

How do we do this? How did I do this?

Well, I'm sure there are many answers, but I think what helped me was growing up with men and women who personified the balance of both male and female within a single personality.

• *Some were gay men, and many were not.*

• *Some were lesbians, and many were not.*

We need to let go of the stereotypes that keep people in little boxes, categories, and compartments, and keep ignorance alive. We should never fear any of the diverse energies in God's creation, and the blending of sexual natures should be affirmed as a blessing.

PRAYER

Today I know I'm so much more than I appear.
There is a history and diversity to my nature
I am only beginning to experience.
It is both imaginative and creative.
Thank You for the gift I am determined to use
for my wellbeing.

"Who giveth this woman to be married to this man?"
Nobody, thank God!

It's over. It is no longer acceptable in civilized and intellectual circles to treat women as chattel. Like cigarette smoking in public spaces, sexism is over.

The religious and church rituals that helped initiate and prolong sexism in society are also over. Sexism may still be lurking in some *strange* and *dark* caverns of the church, but it's over!

Occasionally we hear the death cries of this dis-ease, and feel sorry for those still afflicted:

• *A woman's duty is to obey her man.*

• *Women are the next stage after children; they need to be directed.*

• *A woman without a man is like a ship without a rudder.*

• *Jesus did not call women to the priesthood. A woman, therefore, can never be a priest.*

• *The head and spiritual leader of the family is the husband. A faithful wife must submit to his authority.*

• *A wife's duty is to obey her husband.*

When we hear this, and I suggest reading it out loud because that way it sounds *even sillier*, and we become amazed by the millions who lived and suffered under this abuse.

For me it is as insane as Hitler's demagogic screams:

• *Jews are vermin.*

• *No Aryan can marry a Jew.*

• *The Jew's sole purpose is to corrupt and disease a race.*

• *It is the destiny of the German race to conquer the world and rule for 2000 years.*

Silly stuff. Strange fantasy, involving blood. Amazing what some people will believe if it is said *often enough and loudly enough.*

But it's over. Thank God.

PRAYER

*Great Healer, I know You are present in our lives
and I believe our cooperation in Your will
for the peoples of the Earth is essential.
Thank You for the gift of choice.*

A healthy marriage is based on partnership.

Sexism has no place in a marriage, or any other relationship. Sexism affirms unequal entities and is counterproductive in all partnerships:

• *Within the Church.*

• *Internationally.*

• *In society.*

• *Ecumenically.*

• *Within Government.*

• *Within the family.*

• *In industry.*

Sexism is disastrous in a marriage because it stops the marriage from happening!

You can have a church service, the priest can bless those involved, you might even receive a beautiful certificate that is engraved, framed, and ready to be displayed on the wall, but it is not a marriage.

• *Marriage is based upon partnership.*

• *Sexism is based upon division.*

I expect some of you reading this know exactly what I am speaking about because sexism destroyed your relationship. I hear from so many people the following:

• *From the first night he made me feel unequal, less-than.*

• *If I answered back I was punished.*

• *What was okay for him was not okay for me.*

• *After our marriage, it was clear his energy and affection went to his friends. I was just the wife.*

Sexism is incompatible with marriage, or any healthy relationship. It needs to be confronted, and those afflicted need therapy and ongoing support groups.

We cannot unlearn the messages of a lifetime in a matter of weeks.

PRAYER
I'm willing to look at the unhealthy messages I've received throughout my life concerning the "other sex." I'm ready to let go of the baggage that keeps me arrogant and abusive.

I was opposed to the ordination of women,
not because I was against women,
but because I didn't understand
the totality of Priesthood.

This is a personal statement because it reflects how I felt about priesthood not so many years ago. I was raised to believe *only* men could be priests, because the Church "said so."

Eventually the women's movement came alive within the Church, and many cogent arguments were put forward to cast doubt on this ancient tradition.

Still I felt I needed to *fight* for what had always been the accepted norm, repeating old arguments that seemed to make less and less sense:

• *Jesus called only men to be apostles.*

• *The Holy Spirit guides the Church; therefore, what the Church dictates is God's Will.*

• *Who am I to know better than scholarly bishops?*

• *Women would not be accepted in many congregations.*

• *Women who want to serve God in the Church can become nuns.*

Then I met women who felt called by God, and they posited counter-arguments that enabled me, in good conscience, to change my mind.

For example:

• *Jesus called only Jews but every race is represented in the priesthood today. Why not women?*

• *The Holy Spirit is about change. Perhaps the Holy Spirit is guiding the women's movement in the Church and God wants femininity included in the priesthood.*

• *Many of the women who argued for the ordination of women were scholars educated in theology.*

• *Congregations need to change and grow. We don't want to be seen as God's frozen people.*

• *Being a nun is an excellent vocation, but it is not priesthood. The sacraments are gifts from God that women can interpret in their unique way.*

Priesthood speaks of an inclusive God to the world; this surely includes and involves women!

PRAYER

Today I believe Truth is evolving, and this includes
our understanding of priesthood.
As I grow in my understanding
of Your will for the world,
so I become open and receptive to change.

Sexists are ignorant people because they often keep repeating "tradition" and "how things used to be" without thinking whether what was said *really* made sense. Buried within the ignorance is an insecurity that depends on rules to maintain power and control.

Men feeling superior by making women feel inferior. Often the sexism is subtle, but it is *real*:

• *A man's role is to take care of the woman.*

• *Women are not equipped psychologically for business and negotiation.*

• *A woman's role is not to lead; rather, she is to nurture.*

• *It is not fair to men to have women in the armed forces.*

• *When a man gets in a car with a woman, he should ask to drive. She will have less anxiety if he drives, and will feel more secure.*

• *God created woman to support a man. Her role is to be submissive.*

None of the above is true. But if you keep repeating nonsense enough, you will eventually come to believe it. Ignorance always creates abuse.

What must we do?

Confront it whenever we hear it. With gentle confrontation we can address the ignorance and show it for what it is: prejudice.

While it is true women can exhibit sexist attitudes toward men, they appear to do so less often.

• *A man is not good with children.*

• *It is the nature of men to be aggressive.*

• *Men find it difficult to exist and prosper without a woman.*

• *Men are only big children. They need constant supervision.*

Ignorance is ignorance is ignorance. It is abusive and shaming because it oversimplifies and disregards the variety all people, regardless of sexuality, bring to the table of life.

We all need to work together to let go of the things that keep us divided and ignorant.

PRAYER

God of Truth, You call us to move away
from ignorance to enlightenment.
But we must be willing to begin the journey
by letting go of traditions
hat keep us ignorant.

Sexism manifests as one group of people
feeling powerful at the expense of another.
If one half of the human race believes the other half
is less than, then we have madness.

The world is a healthier place today because sexism is less and less pervasive. More women are involving themselves in every form of profession and opportunity, and our collective creativity and productivity is increasing proportionately.

Spirituality affirms this inclusiveness and promises a world of quantum health and vitality, where a father can say to his daughter:

• *You have unlimited possibilities.*

• *You are an equal child of God with the same opportunities as your brother.*

• *It is important for you to ensure your needs are met. You are free to experience all aspects of life.*

• *As a woman, you bring dignity and genuine strength to this planet. Use it wisely and prudently.*

• *I am so proud of you, my daughter. The New Millennium will begin with the Century of Woman.*

Sexist madness does not comprehend when you abuse one half the human race, you abuse the other half! When a woman is held back simply because she is a woman, then humanity takes a step backwards.

Madness.

PRAYER

I am healing my sexist madness on a daily basis.
And I am excited about future possibilities when
men and women, together holding hands,
march forward.

I've reached the age when I need to let go of most everything I was told about the opposite sex.

We are set up to hate. We are set up to be bigots. We are set up to be sexists:

- *Women are this... men are that...*
- *Don't ever trust a ...*
- *When you find a partner, be sure to keep them on a short leash.*
- *Remember, they're not the same as us. Don't ever forget that.*
- *Don't give them too many compliments, otherwise they will think they are "big shots," something they can never be.*

I'm continually surprised, in a wonderful way, at my interactions with women. The *diversity* and *difference* is staggering. And I was not prepared for it.

I was raised to see women "as my mother," and I was constantly using her as my measuring stick. Few measured up to this unreasonable expectation!

Then some years ago I *processed into letting go* of this expectation. And I am so grateful. Not that I wish to criticize my mother, but women are *more* than my mother.

Variety, temperament, color, personality, education, style, and spiritual insights — women are fascinating and mysterious. Beautiful. Thank Heaven.

PRAYER

God, You certainly knew what You were doing
when You created woman. The mystery of Eve.
And the joy of being Adam.

Wo-man is only man with a wo,
and isn't the wo wonderful!

I feel sorry for people who are sexist, because they miss so much.

I enjoy the company of men, and I find the *competitive stretching* satisfying, but I *love* the company of women. I learn so much about feelings, nature, acceptance, physicality, and specific insights into spirituality.

Women enable me to be a man. A *real* man.

• *Women have taught me to feel, and not fear my expression of those feelings.*

• *Women have introduced me to the gentler insights of God, helping me live with the paradox of divinity.*

• *Women mirror aspects of my nature. I am stronger for being in touch with my femininity.*

• *Women reveal a passive aspect of love that is strong, and an active love that is gentle.*

God, I've discovered so much in the *wo.*

Recently I was helped by a woman priest while counseling a mother to establish boundaries with her two sons. I said she *needed to let go.*

Rev. Eve gently eased herself into the conversation, recognizing how hard it is for a mother to do *anything* that has the appearance of hurting her children. At some point she held the woman's hand, as I slowly stepped aside.

The Rev. Eve continued, gently:

God loves us enough to let us go. God cares enough to give us freedom, and doesn't keep interfering! Maybe that's the model for you and me. Love your sons enough to let them go. Establish boundaries that affirm their freedom. Then, <u>don't interfere</u>.

A woman talking to a woman. Rev. Eve had made connection. She allowed her femininity to empower her priesthood. This is the power of the *wo*!

PRAYER

In the many women I meet, I see a reflection of myself.
They help me nurture the feminine side of my nature.
And I am stronger for it.

Man is woman without the wo.
This is the key to relationship.

We are not the same. The key to the creative vitality of a heterosexual relationship is the difference between a man and a woman. But it is a difference based upon equality. Sexism ruins the potential of relationship.

By making the other sex less than, inferior, or unhealthily dependent, it creates the basis for all manner of abuse:

- *Domestic violence*
- *Religious abuse*
- *Sexual abuse*
- *Economic discrimination*
- *Codependency*
- *Emotional toxicity*

The affirmation of *difference* emphasizes the complementary nature of the man-woman relationship. It is this *mystery* that creates and sustains the love.

Comments I have heard at workshops confirm the above mutuality:

• Jane brings to our marriage the sensitivity and gentleness I need and respect.

• I fell in love with my husband when I discovered his vulnerable strength, which is different from my personal self-confidence. He is a strong man who is able to share his feelings.

• *The children joined us in celebrating our twenty-fifth wedding anniversary. In the after-dinner speeches, my son acknowledged the different love and direction he received from his mother. He shared how he was able to go to his mother with problems she could better understand. But he also celebrated the father-son relationship that was complementary.*

• *Hard to put into words. We all need the different shades of love that exist in a family.*

• *When I met my husband, I knew we had a combined energy that grew in relationship. Nowhere is this more apparent than when we make love. We fit together as one.*

As a man I celebrate the power of the *wo*.

PRAYER

God, You certainly knew what You were doing
in the creation of male and female.
Together we radiate the variety of energies
that exist within You.

God contains the creative elements
of male and female.
Reflection.

I sometimes hear metaphysical people say, "*I am perfect.*" As an Episcopalian priest, this is a new concept to me. When I first heard the remark I dismissed it as being decidedly "Pollyanna-ish."

Then I allowed the poet in me to breathe, and I began to feel the wisdom of the affirmation:

• *Something of the perfect God exists in creation and needs to be acknowledged and celebrated.*

• *The spiritual connection I have with God is All Knowing and All Powerful. When I am aware of this connection, perfection radiates in my life.*

• *For years religion told me what I was not. Spirituality seeks to heal this wound by affirming my perfect nature.*

• *When I love, I enter into the perfect light that radiates from the Creator. It is this energy that has made my marriage creative and healing.*

The constant interaction and interconnection of male and female, based upon *respect*, allows for human perfection to breathe within creation, and *it feels good.*

The human chemistry ignites to make miracle.

We need to let go of the sexist baggage that suffocates this energy and keeps us forever in the dirt!

PRAYER

With my hand firmly grasping Yours,
I walk the path of Perfect Love that is prepared for me.
In the bonding with my soul mate, I am healed.

I'm letting go of the harmful and negative stereotypes.

For years I identified myself by what I was not:

- *I am not a foreigner.*
- *I do not share the beliefs of non-Christians.*
- *I do not know what it feels like to be sexually abused.*
- *I cannot identify with the Women's Movement.*
- *I cannot understand violent people.*

A sponsor told me I could not identify because I was not *hearing, seeing,* or *sharing* feelings! After a period of feeling judged and misunderstood, I revisited my sponsor's remarks and absorbed the message. For years I had felt lonely because I separated myself with a thousand and one disclaimers. Only when I hear, see, and feel do I connect with other people, regardless of culture, religion, or sex. Discrimination is skin deep.

PRAYER

I let go of superficial distinctions that feed my arrogance and false pride. When I allow myself to experience another person, I feel connected.

When I first received communion from a woman priest,
I felt liberated.

A priest repeated the words Jesus had spoken to the disciples: "This is my body… This is my blood…"

But the energy was different. The words were spoken by a woman—a woman priest! I felt *strangely* liberated.

• *It was like Rosa Parks sitting at the front of the bus.*

• *It was like witnessing two gays holding hands on a busy sidewalk, and everybody else going about their business.*

• *It was like seeing the old photograph of Gandhi deep in sincere conversation with the Muslim leader Jinah.*

The woman priest complemented the image of Jesus on the cross. It felt *so right*. Why had it taken so long? Thank God the sexism that has existed in the Church for so long is beginning to heal, and the liberation of Christian women has begun.

PRAYER

Great Creator, I'm increasingly aware of the feminine energy within You. It radiates the acceptance of Your whole creation. It feels strangely liberating. Amen.

An aspect of unhealthy religion is its treatment of women.
However, spirituality is based upon sexual equality.

A poetic nun gave a lesson during a retreat in which she said something I've never forgotten: "The sexism in the Church has deeply wounded the heart of God. And God weeps for the world's loss."

Women do not get a chance to bring the variety of their gifts into the priesthood. Men are deprived through a tragic absence of the feminine energy of divinity.

Women have always been involved in the Church and nobody can deny the powerful role they have played in the development of Christianity. At the same time, there has always been a *glaring absence*.

Still today, in the largest Christian denomination, women are not authorized to be priests. And we all lose.

The nun went on to share at the retreat:

I have felt called to the priesthood since my early twenties. When I spoke to my religious superior, I was punished for my obstinate pride. Still an awareness of the sacred calling grew in my soul. I was led to a Jesuit who told me, "You bear

the baggage of ignorance. Sister, I recognize your Priesthood."
Then he asked for a blessing.

My wounds are being healed by a spiritual community that reminds me to let go of the negative and embrace the positive.

Everybody at the retreat received communion from the nun.

PRAYER

Wounded Healer, I cannot press on without
letting go of the religious baggage
that held my spiritual-self hostage.
I am fortified by the prophetic refrain:
"Let my people go."

Sickness

Chapter 7

Today I'm realizing I am more than my disease.

Many people diagnosed with a sickness allow the condition to overwhelm their thinking and become "who they are." Energy is given to the disease, and this does not help their therapy or recovery.

I have personal knowledge of this. In 1977 I was diagnosed, after a series of alcohol-related accidents and incidents, as an "alcoholic." I came home thinking, "My life is over."

I continued to obsess about my alcoholism, allowing it to consume my energy and thinking. For too many months I felt everybody in the small town of East Grinstead was talking about Fr. Leo's "drinking problem." Of course, they were not.

Then a friend pulled me aside and said, "You are more than your disease."

"I know that!" I brusquely replied.

"Then why are you acting as if your alcoholism means everything to you? All you complain about is being an alcoholic. But you are so much more."

He was right. Soon I started to do other things like playing tennis, enjoying sailing, and entertaining friends over dinner with fizzy lemonade. I began to use my alcoholism to connect with spirituality.

Later I began writing popular books about spirituality and healing. Then followed books about religious abuse issues. Today I'm writing *The Wisdom of Letting Go.*

We are more than any *one* thing. We are certainly more than any disease.

PRAYER

Great Spirit, I am aware of the power
of energy in the Universe.
The power of energy is manifest by
our focus and concentration.
I am unwilling to give spiritual energy to
sickness or negative thinking.

The denial around my acceptance of having cancer
was greater than my denial about being alcoholic.
Probably because I feel so helpless.

In my lifetime, the *Big C* was the scariest thing on the planet, before AIDS came along. It seemed throughout my family there had been cases of cancer, but nobody had called it that. It was:

• *She died from a growth.*

• *A tumor ate him up.*

• *He smoked and did not eat; wasted away.*

• *At forty-seven, God called her home.*

Nobody talked about cancer.

I did not want to think about cancer. I did not want to give energy to cancer. If I had cancer, I didn't want to know.

It was the fear that dare not speak its name.

As bad as alcoholism was, people at least recovered! Twelve Step meetings were filled with people who had twenty, thirty, forty years of recovery.

Cancer? Not good!

The Wisdom of Letting Go

Then I realized my feelings concerning cancer reflected my hopelessness. I had given up on ever recovering from cancer. I had given my spiritual power away.

I needed to let go of this attitude. I believe today we have a spiritual component as human beings that is an *energy healer*, but it requires acceptance. It is hard to bring the God-given power of prayer, meditation, and energy to something we deny.

I make whole what I am willing to face!

I needed to let go of my denial and face the facts.

• *There are effective treatments for cancer.*

• *People are in remission.*

• *Many people live long and effective lives with the disease.*

• *We will all die of something. Let's not make cancer into death. It is a disease.*

PRAYER

Lord, I have found a safe place where I can talk
about my fear concerning cancer.
And I am being healed.
Healed of my ignorance!

When Frank told me he had AIDS,
although I'd been a friend for over fifteen years,
I wanted to just run away.
I didn't want to face him.

Today I know this attitude is about me. Shame is indeed toxic. All the talk and publicity about AIDS being connected with homosexuals, drug addicts, and "low-life" behavior made me run from a friend. A friend I had known for fifteen years. A friend who needed me.

Shame created a codependent cowardice in my life.

• *I was worried about what people might think.*

• *What the neighbors might say.*

• *Would people think I had AIDS?*

• *Why did he have to look so gaunt? I'd invite him to stay at my house if he didn't look so sickly.*

God, did I hate my shame. I hated my cowardice. A priest ran away from a sick person in need — a sick friend in need.

Then I confronted me. I needed to confront my disgusting behavior and discover where it was coming from.

It was all about my fear of my sexuality. My shame over my sexual exploits. The haunting shadow that asks, "Do you have AIDS? How do you know? Even doctors don't know."

It was never about Frank!

Thank God I was able to see Frank before he died. I made my amends. Only then could I let go.

Today I feel Frank *present* in my life, especially when I am in touch with my cowardice.

PRAYER

God of Eternal Strength,
I seek to place my hand in Yours.
It is not easy to confront my fears, cowardice, or shadow.
Yet in the exposure of the feelings is the healing.

I'm realizing shame was my enemy.
Only when I let go of my shame
do I become my friend.

I'm sure I had an investment in *appearing* perfect. It was all so important for me to:

- *Be on time.*
- *Always look clean, tidy and my hair in place.*
- *Never sick or tired.*
- *Never needy.*

When I reflect on this, I see I was ashamed of being human. Why? Many reasons, but I think the toxic religious messages played an important part in this crazy attitude.

Being forced to admit I was alcoholic years ago changed all the above. I needed to let go, and let God.

It wasn't long before I had moved from talking about how I drank, the effects and chaos, to the shame that had lurked my childhood from a young age.

- *I drank in shame.*
- *I used alcohol to run from my shame.*
- *It was shame that fueled my escape into fantasy.*

I knew I needed to let go of my shame if I truly wanted get healthy. But how?

• *I started talking about my childhood, and "stuff" began to surface. Things that had been buried for years began to take on new meaning.*

• *I began to examine the feelings that were involved in my significant relationships.*

• *I started writing a journal. Amazing where my mind drifted.*

• *I drew pictures depicting how I envisioned my place in the family and the world.*

It wasn't too long before I was face to face with my shame. I kissed my shame. Hugged my shame. And then said *goodbye*!

Occasionally my shame returns. But only for a weekend visit!

PRAYER

Resurrected Spirit, I'm realizing we must die to the unhealthy parts of ourselves in order to live the spiritual life. We need to allow ourselves to feel the death of our shame.

What have I done?
Am I to blame for my child's AIDS?
These were the questions I asked
when I first heard the news.

Sickness is often fed by blame.

• *I should have done this or that.*

• *How could I be so stupid?*

• *I'm so selfish. I hurt everyone who is special in my life.*

• *If only I'd done such-and-such, then none of this would have happened.*

• *I'm not a good mother. If I were a good mother my child would not be so sickly, so damaged.*

The "blame game" is about shame!

Life is not about everything going perfectly. We are not God. We don't know everything. Everyone inherits and develops a shadow. Bad things happen to good people.

Essentially I believe we are all "good," carrying a spark of the divine in our natures. However, life brings with it *pain* and *rejection*. As a humorist once said, "None of us gets out of life *alive*."

AIDS is a disease. Nobody wants to have AIDS. People make unwise and unhealthy decisions and — *Wham* — the disease is born! None of us is perfect. We need to learn to let go of shaming judgments.

Healing comes with forgiveness. I believe in a forgiving God. And I seek to reflect that energy in my life.

There is more to life than what we experience on Earth, and I seek to envision a child with AIDS surrounded by a perfect, healing light. The child's destiny is love.

We all need to broaden our horizons so we may move beyond the blame into the healing energy of forgiveness.

PRAYER

I see a sickly child surrounded by a healing light.
In the midst of the suffering I know all is well.
Your love surrounds all Your people.

Not only is my biological system vulnerable to every virus, my whole being is vulnerable to surrounding judgments. Now vulnerability has become my strength. People who had hidden feelings for years are now able to talk with me. My disease has helped create true friendships.

I knew a young man who never felt loved or accepted in his family. He was gay. Always there seemed to be a distance in his relationships at home, especially with his father.

At twenty-one he escaped this atmosphere and moved to Los Angeles. He stayed in touch with his family, but only by telephone, maybe two or three calls a year. This is his story:

He was diagnosed with AIDS. He was determined to keep his sickness from his family. Living alone, he felt extremely isolated but he could not reach out to his family. He felt he would be judged. On one telephone call his mother sensed something was wrong. She told his father. They decided to visit him, but he did not know they were coming.

When they arrived, his father was at a loss for words. Then something triggered within him, and he hugged and kissed his son. Never before had he hugged and kissed his son like he did on this first visit to the one-room apartment.

The Wisdom of Letting Go

The parents decided to stay on. His mother was close by in a motel, and he shared his small apartment with his father. Transformation. The father nursed his son into death, lovingly.

When I visited the young man, he shared something I truly understood: "This disease brought me a gift. My father's love."

PRAYER

Today I am able to view sickness as a different kind of experience life "mysteriously" bestows on all of us. How we respond to sickness is the key to healing.

The stigma of AIDS was my prison.
It bound and gagged me. I felt trapped.
But stigma is in the head, not the heart.
I opened my heart and felt imprisoned no longer.

I'm concerned we become toxic by the poisonous messages we allow to converse in our head.

Many of these messages carry the "virus" of religious abuse:

• *God will punish all gay people.*

• *AIDS is a sign of God's judgment.*

• *The God of scripture is a judging God. Watch out. You never know when He will strike.*

• *Only when you repent from the wretched life you have lived as a homosexual will you be forgiven. Hell is filled with the unrighteous.*

God only knows how many people suffered in isolated rooms, filled with guilt, shame, and remorse, feeling unloved and unlovable—because of the poisonous religious rhetoric of a few homophobic ministers.

The stigma has been as painful as the disease.

We must let go of this *excessive* God of judgment and hate if we are ever to bring healing to all of God's people.

And I do not believe I'm being Pollyanna when I say, "the God of love is surely a God of understanding, diversity, and acceptance." I'm convinced the Jesus I've experienced in the scriptures would be kneeling at the side of an AIDS sufferer, ministering love, healing, and nurturing spirituality. Freedom in death can only come with acceptance.

PRAYER

I know the things that suffocated my spirit
existed in my mind.
Today I'm able to live and love with a freedom
that is grounded in God's acceptance of who I am.

"Why me?" I yelled in anger.
I fought, kicked, and screamed, "Why me?"
"Because you're strong enough to carry it and move on,"
whispered the voice inside.
This voice understands THE MORE.

It is not unusual, and certainly it is understandable, to be angry when we are first diagnosed with a sickness. "Why me?" is something we've all uttered at one time or another.

But as many have commented: "Why not you?" Sickness is not personal; it is a fact of life. We all get sick at some time.

A key to dealing with sickness is *attitude*. When I get the flu, or a heavy cold, I normally take advantage of the sickness. I tell myself my body needs rest. I stay in bed and get plenty of sleep. I catch up on my reading. I use to sickness to my benefit.

I've known people who adopt a similar attitude when they've been diagnosed with cancer or AIDS. It may sound difficult, and it surely is, but what is the alternative? Just roll over and die?

I've known people to read up about the disease, study the various aspects of treatment, and learn more about the human body.

Also, in the face of sickness, they develop a spiritual attitude that sends a positive energy to *envelop* the disease:

- *Courses of meditation.*
- *Use of herbal medicines.*
- *Visualization techniques to affirm the disease being healed.*
- *Religious and spiritual healing services.*
- *Attitude re-adjustment.*
- *Diet experimentation and exercise.*

What many people discover when they seek the above is the *human spirit* is stronger than they ever thought possible. The focusing, on a daily basis, of positive attitudes brings a change in the *feeling* toward the disease. Some speak of actually loving the disease, of embracing and hugging the sickness. Acceptance.

Some begin to heal. Many are in remission. Others die a spiritual death, at peace with themselves and others.

PRAYER
You have invited me into the process of a miracle.
We must be involved in the healing.
Today I understand both life and death
require my full cooperation.

I seek to live a positive attitude
in sickness and in health.

For many years I've suggested to my workshop audiences that spirituality is being a positive and creative person. Spirituality is not merely our attitude toward God; it also involves our attitudes toward ourselves. Especially when we are sick.

So often I've discovered when I'm not feeling well I develop a negative attitude and allow myself to become *depressed*.

• *I go down in my spirit. I progressively become less.*

• *I turn away from the sources of my pleasure.*

• *I isolate from friends who would cheer me up.*

• *I use my tiredness as an excuse to avoid meditation and prayer.*

• *I become a wastebasket of negativity.*

The scary thing about this process is I know I'm doing it. Often I catch myself observing my destructive habits and I make the excuse that I am helpless.

This is not true.

Fortunately, I'm usually able, by the third day, to perform an intervention on myself. Then it's not too long before I'm out of bed and back among my friends.

Life really is about attitude. If we allow the sickness or disease to determine who we are, then we have truly given away our power. When we give away our spiritual power, we become lost.

We should not be codependent in our relationship to sickness and disease. The spiritual attitude of being positive and creative is surely the key to healing and ongoing prevention.

God is on my side, so why am I complaining?

PRAYER

I discover so much of Your power when I have
a positive attitude.
Your creativity requires my Yes to life.
This always includes me.

The pain is unbearable. I want to escape. I want to die!

No, I'm feeling this pain because I don't want to die.

More than anything, I want to live!

As with everything we discuss in this book, a key to healing and spiritual power is our willingness to let go of old tapes. This is certainly true concerning sickness.

- *The doctors say there is little hope. It must be a lost cause.*

- *Nobody dances with cancer and survives.*

- *AIDS is a death sentence.*

- *After the diagnosis he became so desperate he went to church. But I fear God cannot help him now.*

- *If mainstream medicine doesn't work, nothing can help.*

- *Pain is the sword of death.*

We must let go of these depressing and fatalistic attitudes. These tapes tell us to give up in life. And they are not true!

- *Many, many people have lived after doctors had given up.*

- *We would all be surprised at the numbers of people who have survived cancer.*

- *Many people are most active with AIDS. Some are in remission.*

- *Prayer plays a positive role in attitude adjustment. This is essential to healing.*

- *People are discovering in herbal and ancient cultural medicines what they could never find in Western medicine.*

- *Pain is our friend. It usually locates the disease.*

If we keep playing the depressing and disempowering tapes, we will remain depressed and disempowered. There are healing energies beyond our imaginings. We need only seek and ask.

PRAYER

In my affirmation, "I want to live," there is an implied action: I must be willing to live a positive lifestyle.

You are concerned not only with the purity of my morals, but also the quality of my lifestyle.

I was too, too proud of my independence.
There was no one I truly needed, or so I thought.
Now I'm dependent. I have learned to trust.

When we are born, we need help and support. When we prepare to die we also need help and support. Both birth and death are *intimately personal*, yet neither is pursued in isolation! We all need people.

I'm sure there are many reasons we seek independence, and at some level independence is good and healthy. But to feel we don't need anybody is something else.

Probably fear. We fear being rejected so we prefer to go it alone. I know for many years of my life I was too, too proud. I was lonely but I would not ask for help. Even when I was terribly sick in my alcoholism, I still would not pick up the telephone to ask a friend for help. A lonely, miserable priest, who was *insanely* independent!

For many years in my recovery I was isolated and removed. Not drinking, but still feeling alone. I molded my independence into pride, and lost.

You see, I had a sickly independence. It only served to keep me separate and alone.

How did I let go? Well, I'm not sure I have, *completely*. But I began to let go when I felt the pain of loneliness. If left untreated, it is a killer disease. Me. Myself. And no one else! Deadly.

Today I know I am healthily dependent upon friends, family, and recovering folk. I need them. Life would be empty without them. The love I have discovered today enables me to ask for help. And it feels good.

My fear has been replaced by trust.

PRAYER

As a child I was told You were a proud God.
Today I recognize You as a Lover who seeks to be loved.
And sometimes I feel You need us.

I sat in the park today, the one I used to run through on my way to work. I am unable to run anymore.

But I noticed the roots of trees, the scent of flowers, and the songs of various birds. Everything is real and available to me now. Being old in years is a blessing.

I once visited an elderly woman in a retirement home, who complained for nearly an hour.

• *I hate this place. Nobody has time to talk with you.*

• *The food and the dining room are constantly a mess.*

• *My bones ache. I can't move. It's terrible when you get old.*

• *The only thing worse than being old, is being surrounded by older people!*

• *God has a wicked sense of humor. He makes you pay for your life with old age.*

After a while, she was interrupted by an old man wearing a blissful smile. He had a different experience of the same place.

• *Every day he had visitors, and the caregivers were delightful and courteous.*

• *He enjoyed the food and appreciated not having to cook and clean up.*

• *He appreciated how age brings a sea of memories. He earned every painful joint.*

• *His friends in the retirement home were like walking, talking encyclopediae. One woman was born in the early 1900s.*

• *Today is the time to smell the roses. For many, old age is a sickness; for others, a blessing.*

PRAYER

Thank You for this thing we call attitude,

this inner focus that can lead to resentment or happiness.

Life, even when we come close to death,

requires a healthy attitude.

I remember people saying, "Helplessness is a weakness."
Today I believe helplessness prompted me to search within
myself and discover my creativity.

I remember an old priest telling me spiritual persons can see the good and the beautiful in everything. They can turn an apparent negative into a positive.

We need to be willing to let go of the idea of *permanency*.

• *I am weak, so I will remain, all my life, helpless.*

• *I am angry, so I will remain abusive.*

• *I am alcoholic, so I will remain worthless and alone.*

• *I am depressed, with mental anxiety, so I will remain sick.*

It is the challenges in life that take us to our spiritual power points, creating a deeper appreciation of what it means to be human. Nurturing a respectful empathy for the suffering of others accomplishes this as well.

And nothing need remain permanent. If we are willing to face the "dark side" of our life, confront the shadow, seek to understand the energy that feeds it, then we can *turn it around*.

"I once was lost, but now I'm found," is a theme with which most human beings can identify at some time in their lives. Those who cannot identify are really lost!

PRAYER

God, I'm discovering even my apparent helplessness
can be an opportunity for growth and healing.
My vulnerability is the pathway to
my spiritual strength.

I was crippled by fear, terrified for the future.
Fear was holding me back. It always had.
Afraid of doing or saying the wrong thing.
This realization became the key to my healing.

I remember hearing somebody say, "He was a coward in life, and now he's a coward in death!"

Fear is a strange feeling. It comes from a multitude of places. But always we *learn* fear:

• *God is watching you. When you do something wrong, you'll get zapped.*

• *Don't ever try to be bigger than your boots.*

• *Better to be safe than sorry.*

• *The world is a frightening place, so don't upset too many people.*

• *Better the devil you know, than the devil you don't.*

It's hard to be strong when you're always afraid.

Then somebody says face the fear. Confront the bogeyman. Why spend your whole life in a prison created by "what if?"

Certainly when we are sick we need to confront our fear, or we will give up before we have a chance to work the steps to healing. I know this to be true. For too many years I was afraid to tell anybody my drinking was out of control. They knew. But nobody wanted to say anything. The pink elephant was in the front room and everybody tiptoed around it. *Fear*.

Then there was a crisis. A moment. A car crash. And I actually saw what I had been denying for years.

This realization became the key to my healing. If we keep giving energy to the fear, it grows into an elephant! But there are always opportunities that cross our path, and these opportunities offer the key to freedom. Usually the opportunities come with the fear. Emotional. Physical. Mental. The pain stimulates courage to move, shout, change, or simply get honest.

Overcoming the fear is the key to healing.

PRAYER

God, for too many years I feared You, and I missed You.
I feared others, and I was lonely. I feared myself,
and I grew sickly. Then came the pain.
And with the pain came the choice. I took a risk.
Now I'm really alive.

The numbness I originally felt turned to apathy.
Apathy proved to be a greater sickness than HIV.
Letting go of apathy empowered me to seek treatment.

Sometimes life seems so difficult, so painful, that we become numb.

- *We stare, but we do not see.*
- *We listen, but we do not hear.*
- *We speak, but say nothing.*
- *Feelings drift into a deathly numbness.*

Apathy is really scary because it has no visible symptoms that are easy to detect. Apathy is life imitating a zombie!

How do we snap out of this? It's not easy.

Certainly for those with HIV or AIDS, the temptation to drift away, isolate, and prepare a place to quietly die is enormous.

How do we let go of apathy? Something has to shake us up. Knock us off kilter. Create a wakeup call.

What?

• *Maybe a friend being real. Expressing anger not at our sickness, but our attitude.*

• *Perhaps a book, tape, or movie mirrors something back to us that reminds us we are more than the disease.*

• *A "seeing" of ourselves, not just physically, but spiritually, and how we have allowed ourselves to be beaten without putting up a fight.*

• *A God-experience that requires our involvement.*

A friend wrote me of an event that changed his life:

He has HIV. He had given up. Then in a park he saw a small bird that had been ravaged by a cat. It was fighting to breathe. Fighting to fly. Fighting to live. He took the bird home and nursed it for many days. The wounds eventually healed. it was miraculous to watch. One day the bird flew away. he realized it was a God-experience. The bird brought a message. He needed to fight to live.

Miracle.

PRAYER

You are all around. I've heard that said for years and only recently has it come to mean something. Why?
Because now I'm actually looking for You in Creation.

AIDS is not a punishment from God. My family was wrong to say that! I'm a human being who wanted to love and be loved. No more. No less. I'm not angry at the person who transmitted the disease to me. I'm just sad.

Sometimes life is sad.

- *Things are said in ignorance that hurt and confuse.*
- *People get angry and say things they don't really mean.*
- *Precautions are not taken.*
- *A sick person, in genuine ignorance, passes on the disease.*

Sadness.

Religious abuse is real. It tells you what you are not, but rarely tells you who you are. It places an unnatural emphasis on sin, guilt, shame, hell, and punishment, but rarely does it balance the "hate rhetoric" with an emphasis upon love, acceptance, freedom, spiritual healing, and joy.

AIDS is not a punishment from God for being homosexual. It is tragic some Christian ministers have said such things, or allowed their preachments to imply such conclusions. Denying you *actually* preached such a lie is too late after a suicide.

AIDS, as with other diseases, requires medicine and *Love. Love in abundance.*

A friend who suffered from AIDS and is now in the healing process wrote this:

I was raised to feel guilty about my sexuality. However, once I left home, I connected with a metaphysical church that combined a healthy attitude with scripture and science. Both were seen as part of revelation.

Once I was diagnosed with AIDS, I told the congregation at a prayer meeting and received unconditional love from everyone. I took my medicine, but I also surrounded myself with positive affirmations and healing tapes. I envisioned the disease leaving my body. I saw it consumed by light.

On a daily basis I sought to let go of negative attitudes and destructive behaviors. I proclaimed healing and wellness in my life. My shout created a miracle. I'm in remission.

PRAYER

Today I know sadness is a feeling we can move beyond if we have a positive attitude.
It's okay to be sad, but sadness is not who I am.

When I contracted HIV, I thought myself stupid.
Now I have a knowledge beyond most
and I've become an educator.

It's amazing how something seen initially as a curse can become a blessing.

• *Alcoholism, when accepted, becomes a source of wellbeing and prosperity.*

• *Divorce offers an opportunity for new love.*

• *Cancer brings the key to a spiritual search that leads to an inner peace.*

• *HIV can be the beginning of a healthy lifestyle, an awareness of being human and having challenges, and the opportunity to serve, in a unique way, the needs of others.*

We are beginning to read more and more about the importance of the shadow in our lives, the primal side of our nature that few people are willing to talk about. It is in our shadow nature that *disease* has a special place because it gets mingled with fear, mortality, sexuality, and our animal instinct.

However, if we are able to confront our disease and speak about all the feelings that surround it, then we become aware of who we are in a most special way.

It's trite but true: *Disease presents challenges that lead to growth.*

To face and live with a disease on a daily basis, inviting it into our shadow nature, and making it a friend, is a unique life experience.

Most teachers have at some time been forced to confront their shadow, and we all are the beneficiaries.

PRAYER

Today I am able to recognize the gift my disease brings.

Healing and recovery have their roots in my shadow.

I lived on junk food.
Exercise was for fitness-freaks and movie stars!
Now I'm fitter than ever. What's my secret? HIV.
I was a slob. Now I'm a survivor.

It really is amazing what can happen to a person who comes face to face with death. Some people give in, surrender in apathy, and pathetically await what they see as the inevitable.

And others fight back:

• *The disease created a wake-up call in my head. I may have a disease, but I'm not going to walk toward death like a lamb to slaughter. I'm not going without a fight.*

• *At first I lost myself in booze and cigarettes. Then one morning, for no apparent reason, I decided to go for a walk along the beach. The next morning I went for a jog. Soon I was running and attending a gym. I quit drinking and found a support group for people with HIV. I believe I can live with this disease.*

• *I expected the HIV diagnosis. But I didn't expect my reaction. For years I'd been irresponsible with my life, but now I wanted to live with dignity. I read spiritual books. I found a gay-friendly church. Today I have a God of my understanding. HIV is a blessing!*

It is important to let go of the idea that being HIV positive equals death. Especially today, with the medication "cocktails" available, a person can really survive being HIV positive.

Medical drugs obviously help; in addition, an inner affirming attitude is also required. It's not enough to be positive and creative when things are going well. The real test is to nurture spirituality during the challenging times.

PRAYER

For years I've believed You are the Great Physician.

Today I know You require my involvement in my healing.

I'm learning to co-create on a daily basis.

*My life was so very controlled, well ordered, safe,
with no surprises. The diagnosis of breast cancer
threw everything into turmoil. How could this be?*

The woman whose experience is described above became totally disoriented as a result of her diagnosis. It took her a few months to settle down. Now her journey is focused, but spontaneous. She is living in the moment.

- *You never really know what is going to happen next.*
- *Life is full of surprises.*
- *Live one day at a time.*
- *Let go… and let God.*

There are a hundred different sayings that suggest life and *human control* are not an ideal partnership. Murphy's Law: just when you had everything neatly tied up with a ribbon, something happens to create confusion. Surprise!

Few of us really expect to die. Most of us live in denial of our own mortality. Society, family, and sometimes even the Church shield us from the pain and reality of death. *Then something happens.*

Few are able to envision fatal diseases as a blessing. But there are those who are able to let go of the fear and embrace the adventure, and what they say or write is truly amazing.

• *Each moment is treasured.*

• *No act of kindness is taken for granted.*

• *The small and seemingly inconsequential aspects of nature are a constant source of wonderment.*

• *Even the making of an omelet becomes an act of appreciation!*

PRAYER

I'm trying not to take the gift of life for granted.
I realize I miss so much of Your glory in the
ordinary everyday happenings of life.
Miracles on the sidewalk.

I mourned the loss of friends who abandoned me when
the truth of my disease was known.
And I appreciate the friends who remained.
Today I celebrate and crave the love of family and friends.

People are strange. People who you think you *know*, when sickness strikes, you realize you *do not know*! In sickness, sometimes even friends walk away. Why?

• *Not knowing how to talk about the sickness.*

• *Embarrassment and fear.*

• *Disease makes them uncomfortable with part of their buried selves.*

• *Not able to cope with suffering or death.*

• *Fear of their own mortality.*

Yet there are other friends who offer unconditional love. Sometimes even mere acquaintances grow into "angels of mercy."

A friend who was in the hospital, near death, told me the following story:

I *did not know Mary. She was visiting somebody in the next room, but she always popped in to say a few kind words as she passed by. Each day she stayed a little longer, talking.*

The Wisdom of Letting Go

When her friend in the next room died, Mary continued to visit me. We became friends. She talked about her feelings of grief and loss, about the pain of death.

When I left the hospital, she continued to visit me at home. A stranger had become, in a few short months, my dearest friend. We have a soul connection.

Sickness is a test of *real* friendship, *real* love.

It is smart to let go of any expectations concerning how friends and family will react. Remember, people are *strange*!

PRAYER

God, Your love is absolute and unconditional.
This I believe. However, reality teaches me friends
can let you down; they may walk away in the time of need.
I do not judge. I embrace acceptance.
But I'm grateful for the family and friends
who are able to give love during the testing times.

Death

Chapter 9

I grieved for years because I would not accept my husband was dead. It was years before I cleaned out his cupboards and gave away his clothes.

The healing begins when we become willing to let go.

If you stop to think about it, *we've always lived in life*! That statement seems funny when you write it down, but it is true. When we've only experienced life, how can we imagine or *really think ourselves* into death!

Yet we know people die. We read every day about people being killed. However, it's not really *personal*— it's happening to other people. With this in mind, I can appreciate the above words from a woman who finds it impossible to accept that her husband is dead.

• *We've all been sick, so we can identify with sickness.*

• *We've all been away and returned, so we can identify with long trips.*

• *We've all grown older, so we can identify with the aging process.*

But death is an enigma to the living! When we also consider the fact that few of us are comfortable talking about death, then the "denial" from the wife seems understandable. *Yet death is a fact that we all must face.*

As a priest I've been involved in "death ceremonies" for many years and I know people come to terms with death in many different ways. A few may never come to terms with it. For some, the grieving takes longer than for others. The letting go takes time.

I think it is wise to avoid the *should* mentality:

• *You should be over his death by now.*

• *You should not keep her clothes in the house. get rid of the photographs.*

• *You should be going out and seeing other people.*

• *As a Christian, your faith should be your consolation.*

I'm of the opinion that people accommodate death in a variety of ways. It's not helpful to give guilt to the grieving! As we've explored in this book, love is very different for each person, and so is how we cope with death.

Bless them, love them, hold their hand. Time really is *the healer.*

PRAYER

You are the mystery that continues in death.
I accept that I do not understand death.
Sometimes I fear it; always I respect it.
Today I know death is the tough part of life!

The preacher said death is not the end,
but the door to another life.
Why can't I believe this?

It is so easy to say things, but much more difficult to *feel* and *fully understand* the things we say.

As a preacher, I understand the difficulty most people experience in a funeral service because often the words are written down in a book, or read from the ancient scriptures and, for the people who *really knew* the deceased, it all seems so unreal, so theatrical. And it is. When we attend a funeral service we are involving ourselves in a ritual.

This ritual is supposed to bring consolation. Every religion or culture has a service for the dead that expresses whatever belief *the tribe* has concerning death and the afterlife. Most death ceremonies emphasize *the journey*.

• *We meet here to witness Leo moving beyond the role of life into the bliss of eternity.*

• *As the smoke rises from the funeral pyre, so the spirit of Gandhi rises to the heavens.*

• *We bury the physical body of Sarah, but her spirit continues into the arms of the Creator.*

• *The adventures of White Eagle will continue beyond these flames and he will reunite with his ancestors, the Great Warrior Spirits.*

Some people have no difficulty believing this; others are agnostic.

I understand agnostics and often share their doubts about what religion is saying. Often it seems so cut and dried, so black and white. But when I allow the poet in me to rise up and look beyond the words, beyond the ritual phrasing, then I enter the world of *mystery*.

I take comfort in the fact that the cultures of the world, in different ways with a variety of rituals, all seek to affirm the ongoing adventure of the life force beyond death. It's a collective consciousness, a collective belief energy.

I connect with this.

PRAYER
My spiritual belief today allows me to look beyond
the words of my faith and connect with the
universal Spirit that brings healing and hope.
Death challenges the poet in me to sing.

I'm not afraid of death. I'm afraid of dying.

I hear this statement often from the religious and nonreligious. How we die seems to be the big issue.

This brings together the *connection* between spirituality and death. If you agree being a spiritual person involves developing a positive attitude and creative lifestyle, you know we need to be actively involved in *preventive* health measures:

• *Exercise and healthy food plan.*

• *Rest and involvement with spiritual retreats.*

• *Ensuring our friends and colleagues have a positive attitude.*

• *Therapy treatment for dysfunctional baggage we have inherited from family or religion.*

• *Practicing letting go of issues that are not our responsibility.*

• *Developing a prosperity plan that allows us to cope with health challenges.*

How we die in many cases involves making choices today about how we live. So many illnesses are created by the irresponsible choices we make in life.

The spiritual person takes full responsibility for lifestyle choices and knows we are each responsible for the health we manifest in our lives. Things do not just happen. We determine our life and, in many cases, how we die. If we truly fear the act of dying, then we should start making healthy decisions today.

PRAYER

My relationship with You tells me I am
not a puppet on a string.
I'm responsible for my life,
and this includes how I will die.

There are still so many things I want to do.
I'm too young to die!

It is sad to be facing death early in life. Yet people diagnosed with cancer or AIDS are forced to consider that their life *could* be over at an early age. Is there anything they can do?

We know our attitude plays an important part in coping with an illness. Certainly attitude is crucial to the energy we create as to *how* we die. But being diagnosed with a deadly disease does not in itself mean we will die. It is never good to just "roll over" and await what we consider to be the inevitable.

So many stories abound concerning people diagnosed with a terminal sickness whose positive attitude engendered remission. Saying, "I'm too young to die," can be an apathetic response or a powerful affirmation to fight the sickness. It really is all in the *tone of the voice*. Spirituality is involved in the expression of our feelings.

I remember a young man diagnosed with AIDS telling me he was not going out without a fight. He worked with his physician on a medical plan, but he also attended a Spiritual Center where he was surrounded by positive attitudes and herbal treatments. He lived many years beyond the prognosis.

He died surrounded by a "love energy." His family and friends were at the bedside and he was able to bring closure to any outstanding issues in his life. I was involved in a Service of Transition he had created. I can't remember all he wrote, but I do remember this line:

"I'm ready to go on to the next chapter of my life, grateful for the love and friendship I have experienced in this life."

He died with an attitude of gratitude.

PRAYER

God, You are my partner.
You are also the love energy that pervades this planet.
I want to face each day reflecting this love.
I want to die in love.

I'm not afraid of death.
I believe it to be the beginning
of a wonderful adventure.

Sometimes you meet people who genuinely are not afraid of death. They love life, they take advantage of every second life brings, but at the same time they seem to *know* the adventure of life continues through the door of death.

Eric was such a person. He was in his eightieth year when he died, having had a full life in the British Foreign Service. He had spent many years in India, and when I met him in Brighton, he was preparing for what he called "the death adventure." He was also a recovering alcoholic of over twenty years. He wrote me his thoughts about death:

I'm not afraid to die because I know the spirit that exists within me has lived in other ages at different times. I can't prove it to anybody, but I know it. When I first moved to India, I knew I had lived there before. I had experiences that proved this, for me. I knew I had a very old soul. My religion in this life was Methodist, but today I like to think of myself as spiritual. We can learn something from every religion and culture, if we have an open attitude.

Today this body is ready to go into the "Spiritual Shop." I enjoyed this experience. Really, I'm going to miss so many places and people I take for granted. But I'm ready for the next adventure. Death is my friend. I welcome Him. As I've welcomed Him before. Each challenge I've had in life prepares me for the next life. I've learned I need to respect my body; recovery from alcoholism taught me that. Also, I embrace the mystery of God's energy; India taught me that.

I'm ready to go. Thank you for being my friend.

Love, Eric.

Eric knew about letting go.

PRAYER

Lord, sometimes I fear death.
I think I'm going to miss out on something.
I sometimes lament that life ends in death.
But other times I know life goes on.
People like Eric help me believe beyond my unbelief.

When I watched my father die,
with so many feelings left unsaid,
an opportunity was lost.

The act of dying, because of its apparent finality, brings with it *opportunities*. Many people are propelled to "clear the air" in the face of death, to get the stuff "off their chest" that has been clinging for too long.

Death brings the *time* to clean the slate:

• *I don't want you to die without knowing how much I've loved you. I'm sorry it's taken me so long, but I come from a family that tells me to keep my feelings to myself. I can't do that with you. I don't want to do that with you. Know I love you. There, I've said it.*

• *It's a funny thing to say, but death brought me my mother. I was the daughter who lived a separate life from my parents. This is not the time to explain why, but when my mother was alone and dying I volunteered to nurse her. My mother became my child. For the first time in my life, she needed me. As I held her in my arms I was able to tell her I loved her. Death brought me a gift.*

• *I didn't want what happened when my mother died to happen when my father faced death. I never had closure with my mother. It still pains me. With my father, I went over our times together, the good and the bad, and we were able to forgive each other. He died at peace. I live in peace. Oh yes, he told me he would explain everything to my mother. But I'm also going to write a letter and burn it with my minister.*

We don't always have an opportunity at the time death for closure. What can we do?

• *Write a letter.*

• *Talk everything over frankly with a minister, sponsor, or friend.*

• *Talk – a prayer to the one who died.*

• *Draw a picture of what your completed relationship looks like.*

Then, let go.

PRAYER

Death brings with it a new way to look at life.
It brings the birth of a new adventure not only for
the departed, but also for the living.

As I await death, which I know to be so close,
I sit in my garden and observe so much I missed in life.

It is tragically sad but so many people, as they approach death, realize how much they missed in life.

The poet Davies again comes to mind:

> *What is this life*
> *If full of care,*
> *We have no time*
> *To stand and stare.*

Life is more than work, accumulating money, manipulating relationships, and worrying about what might happen. Life is experience!

Sometimes I take off away from my work and wander along the beach, or organize a picnic in the woods. Always I am appreciative of nature.

So much is given in life that is *free*—it only demands our observation.

As a priest I occasionally visit a person who is close to death, and I am always saddened to hear: "If only I'd…"

As you read this, make a decision to appreciate life in all its fullness:

- *Spend time with family members and those you love.*
- *Begin learning the new language you've always talked about.*
- *Visit a foreign country while you're young enough to appreciate it.*
- *Visit the countryside and appreciate the beauty of nature.*
- *Take time to smell the roses.*

Churchill once said the things that worried him in the night, and kept him awake, *rarely happened*!

The serenity prayer reminds us to create balance in our lives. We accept the things we cannot change, and we develop the courage to change the things we can. We are human *beings*, not human *doings*!

PRAYER

I'm appreciating Your creation in all its fullness.
Today I'm able to watch the rabbits play and the birds fly.
I get up early to see the sun rise and spend time,
in the evening with friends, observing it set.
It truly is a wonderful world.

A fact of life is death.

When I was a little boy, I went with my mother to visit a sick aunt. The following week I was told she had *gone on a journey*. I was confused. I asked if she was coming back. I was told her journey would take a long, long time, but one day I'd see her again.

Within days the family got dressed up in black clothes and left me with a neighbor. They all returned home, crying, but at the same time eating and drinking a lot! The priest was with them. Nobody said anything about *death*.

Some years later I was able to put it all together and I realized that Auntie Beatrice had died, and the adults had gone off to the funeral. They had left me with a neighbor.

- *I felt angry.*
- *Angry I was not told.*
- *Angry I was not included in the funeral service.*
- *Angry I could not say goodbye.*

Why the *secrecy* that surrounds death? Death becomes horrifying in the *silence*. Yet death is an important part of life; it is the other side of birth.

I was recently in Bali, Indonesia and I witnessed a cremation that had been arranged by a local village for an elder. Everybody was there. People cried, sang, ate, and shared stories. The children cried and played throughout the service. It all seemed so natural. Beautiful. Real.

I think so many Westerners have fear and guilt concerning death because we do not look upon it as part of the life cycle; we make it into something "other." It becomes part of a *shameful secret* we find difficulty talking about. Feelings are suppressed; opportunities, lost.

Death is part of the journey in life we all need to face. It often brings an opportunity for closure. It ensures a healthy grief. We should never hide it from the living.

PRAYER

Today I'm able to talk about death.
When I remember those I love who have died,
I'm able to cry.
I tell stories that keep their lives authentic.
Death helps me stay real.

*The thing that makes me angry, as I lie in my dying bed,
is that nobody wants to talk about death!*

These words were said to me when I visited an elderly
woman in her home, a few weeks before she died:

• *She was made to feel ashamed about her pain.*

• *She was not able to bring closure to her full and blessed life.*

• *Her finances and personal arrangements, which she wanted to
share with family, were surrounded by unnecessary secrecy.*

• *In her last weeks, she was forced to be nice when she desperately
needed to be real.*

• *A gift that can only come with death was lost.*

I wonder if she went through the door of death angry.

I was the visiting priest. It was early in my ministry,
and I was out of my depth. I had grown up with the
same *silence* that surrounded death in her family.

I found an *unhealthy security* in the family's
unwillingness to face death. It gave me the "*out*" I was
looking for, so I comforted myself with *nice* prayers that
said *nothing*!

I would not do this today. I've managed to let go of my fear around death. Today I use death to create spiritual connection. Death can be a powerful *healer* in any family.

PRAYER

*I don't want to live in fear, and I certainly
don't want to die in fear.
When I read about Jesus expressing his love
to family and friends before He died,
I experience a spiritual awakening.
Jesus showed us how to live.
He also showed us how to die.*

My nephew, who is only ten,
broke the silence in my hospital room and asked,
"Are you afraid of dying?"

"And a child shall lead them."

It really is amazing how we sometimes need a jolt to wake us up to the things in life that are really important—and we need to talk about. Over the years people have come to me at workshops and said:

• *How can I make amends to mother and father? They died when I was in prison. They never saw me sober. I wasn't able to comfort them.*

• *I felt so much love for my husband as he lay in the hospital bed. I wiped his face, I kept his bed comfortable, I fed him, but I couldn't express my feelings. I kissed him after he'd died.*

• *I was my mother's only daughter. We were close, but not really intimate. I knew she was afraid of dying. I wanted to ease her fears. Talk. I went every night with the intention of beginning a conversation about death. The afterlife. Our Christian faith. But always I remained silent.*

Sometimes I think we're so damn *nice*. So proper. So controlled. So determined not to lose it and cause a scene. Death demands we become real.

Children often say what is on their minds. They've not lived long enough to learn how to stuff their feelings. They live in the moment.

Maybe we all need to discover the child within. Let's let go of the pretense and say what we wanted to say way back then.

It's never too late to speak with Spirit.

PRAYER

You are present with me now,
and You are surrounded by the departed.
oday I am able to pray to you and talk with them.
I cry, get angry, ask forgiveness, and reminisce,
all in a single prayer. I'm connected.

When I was young I thought I would live forever.
Now my life is coming to an end.
It all seems to have happened so very, very quickly.

Life moves very quickly. If you don't really concentrate, you can miss it!

I can identify with the above statement, although I hope I've got plenty of years left in this Episcopal body, because it's hard to believe I'm now in my fifties.

* *I remember being at school as if it were yesterday.*

* *I remember my first kiss. Wow!*

* *I remember the first concerned friend talking about my problematic drinking.*

* *I remember completing my first year of sobriety.*

* *I remember my first week in America, thinking I'd stay about five years. I've been here twenty!*

* *Now I'm developing a financial plan for my retirement.*

I know I'm probably closer to my death than I am to my birth. It's all happened so very, very quickly.

Am I prepared for death? Not in a morbid, resentful way, but in a spiritual sense. Yes, and no.

- *I've completed a Testimony of Will.*
- *I've arranged my funeral service.*
- *I've visited the places on this planet I really wanted to see.*

But I'm not sure I've really said the things I need to say to the people I love.

There are still things I need to let go, in order to be comfortable with my past, and face the future in peace.

I have gratitude moments I need to recall and savor. I don't want death to take me by surprise!

PRAYER

God, I'm ready to embrace the next leg of my journey.
But don't misunderstand me, I'm not eager.
One day at a time I seek to live in gratitude.

These words were spoken by a man in a hospital, when I visited him at the request of his family. He was clear about being responsible for his early death.

- *I smoked and drank far too much. I still smoke.*

- *I never took care of my body.*

- *I ate what I could grab. Never thought about a food plan.*

- *I can't remember when I last took a vacation.*

- *If my body were a car, it would have been in the scrapyard years ago.*

I noticed he had three photographs of his dog. They were his only photographs. *He loved his dog.*

Interesting, he took excellent care of his dog.

- *A walk every night.*

- *Exercise in the day.*

- *The best food.*

- *Heaps of affection.*

As I left the hospital, I knew there was a message in this tragic life.

We destroy what we most love when we mistreat ourselves.

His dog would miss him. His dog was in a pound. Maybe, just maybe, he'd killed his dog.

PRAYER

Because I love my family and friends,
I determine each day to love myself.
I'm not afraid of death. It will come to all of us,
but I don't want to kill myself by
irresponsible actions and choices.
Spirituality teaches me to let go of nonsense.

I don't think I could face the pain of dying
without a sense of spirituality.
I know I'm connected with the ongoing cycle
within this thing we call the universe.

Spirituality is about *connection*. It connects with life. It connects with death. It heals the fear that surrounds our dying, and gives us a glimpse of heaven—*the place of bliss.*

• *Spirituality tells me everything has a reason and there is an energy connection that holds everything together: the good and the bad, light and darkness, mortality and divinity, today and tomorrow, and life and death.*

• *Spirituality tells me although I fear dying, and fear death, everything will be okay. There is a rhythm to life that must include death. I'm not expected to understand it. Rather, I should move toward it with acceptance.*

• *Spirituality tells me all the great religions don't have all the answers, but they have some answers, some insights. Fear is a human response to the unknown. Faith encompasses and holds the transcendent vision. We are blessed with both.*

• *Spirituality connects me with the energy cycle within creation. I am separate, yet mysteriously attached.*

Alice Walker expressed it so clearly, "If you cut the tree, I bleed."

PRAYER

God, I'm beginning to understand spirituality
is the golden thread that connects everything together.
With this belief, I am able to face death.

The things I worried about most in life
now seem so very unimportant.

Death has a way of getting our attention. After birth it is the most important aspect of life because it is:

(a) either the door to nothingness; or

(b) the beginning of a new adventure.

I *believe* it is the beginning of a new adventure. Am I afraid? Some days. Other times I get excited about what it is going to be like. On my most content days I imagine the following:

• *After death I enter a place of perfect peace and serenity. I am usually surrounded by a gentle light.*

• *Family and friends I have loved on Earth are connected to me, and I feel their presence.*

• *Jesus, the Buddha, Mohammed and other great spiritual teachers welcome me and give feedback on my life.*

• *At some point I am informed about an appointment with God. I'm always afraid. The Teachers and my family tell me I have nothing to fear.*

• *I know and feel I am in a better place.*

The above imaginings help me put my life in perspective. It's unwise to plan my life on Earth as if I'm always going to be here, for life on Earth is *spiritually relative*. Houses, jobs, finances, family, friends, lovers, food, sex, garden, and animals — they are all *taking me* and *preparing me* for the journey that begins through death. I cannot build eternal hopes and dreams on *"this life."*

Also my worries, anxieties, fears, and sufferings will end. Do I think I'll come back again as a prince, pauper, frog, or butterfly? Maybe. But eventually I know I shall be in a place my culture calls *heaven*. I'll be ready.

PRAYER

Jesus, I've reached a stage in my life when
I'm thinking about death.
Not obsessively. But sometimes.
And it helps me put everything into perspective.

As I look back on my life,
I don't think I've changed very much.

Sometimes I think I've not changed *so very much*.

Oh yes, I'm older, fatter, grayer, richer, and wiser (sometimes), but the little boy who raced his bicycle down the streets of Salford, Lancashire is still very much alive and present!

• *I still feel life is an adventure and I'm amazed at what I'm able to get away with.*

• *I still find life a mystery, and when I look up at the stars, I know there is a happy God who loves and cares for me.*

• *I know although I have a family and a culture, I'm still independent and separate, with a life only I can live.*

• *I know I do good things and bad things, I have generous thoughts and selfish thoughts, but there are more good things about me than bad.*

• *I know the challenges that faced me as a little boy are still present today, only in different forms. Sometimes I look in the mirror and "little Leo" winks back at me.*

Oh yes, I've changed. But not very much. As Noel Coward said, "Life is a variation on a theme. And each theme is unique."

PRAYER

God, fifty, sixty, seventy years is nothing in Your sight.
A life is but a moment against the backdrop of eternity.
Why, then, should we expect such great changes?

I never thought I would be burying my own son.
It seems so unnatural. So perverse.

Death, for some, comes *too soon*.

How can we cope with a son or daughter dying before their time, when parents are still alive?

For some people spirituality teaches there is not a *right* time to die, only *a* time. People live the time allotted to them. They have done what they needed to do, they have learned what they needed to learn, then they die.

I'm not sure I agree with this. I tend to believe we make healthy and unhealthy choices, and the result can mean prosperity or death.

• *If you continue to smoke cigarettes you will shorten your life.*

• *If you walk in unsafe areas you are more liable to experience violence.*

• *If you continue to take risks with you life, like using drugs or hanging out with violent people, the time will come when you must pay the piper!*

• *If you eat unhealthily and refuse to exercise, the results will probably be sickness and an early death.*

Choice plays an important role in life. It also plays a role in how we die. *And some people die young.*

Parents who bury their children, and do not have a spirituality that includes death, with a belief in the eternal journey, will be particularly wounded and depressed.

• *Accidents occur in life.*

• *Bad things happen to good people.*

• *In a complicated world, we cannot predict tomorrow.*

Talking about death enables us to face it. Only when we learn to live with death and make it our friend will it lose its terror.

PRAYER

God, I do not pray for those who die young.
I know they are journeying to You.
It is the parents and friends I pray into the circle of light,
that they may hold the vision which heals the wounds.

I've read about people dying every day.
I've watched so many die on TV.
Now it's my turn and I hate the world's indifference.

Death is only important to those who are dying, and the family and friends who also feel the pain. But the vast majority of people don't really care. Life goes on.

Amazingly, we watch TV or read a newspaper that records death as we sip a coffee, eat a sandwich, or talk intermittently about a football game.

• *Six people were killed this morning and eight were seriously injured as a gunman went crazy in a supermarket in Palm Springs, California.*

• *More than 300 people were killed and many more injured when a plane crashed at the Manila airport in the Philippines.*

• *A flood washed an entire village away outside Delhi, India this morning. Deaths are said to be in the thousands!*

And the rest of the world sips a coffee, eats a sandwich, or talks intermittently about a football game!

Our lives are personal. But Life is business as usual. The world is indifferent.

There is a spiritual message in this indifference:

- *We must let go of super-ego.*
- *We are not the only game in town.*
- *People grieve only what they know.*

This is the reason it is important to make real connections with family and friends. When we know we are dying, it is healing to share the process, fear, doubts, and regrets with those we love. Death is a private, personal moment that can be a precious gift to only those we love.

PRAYER

Great Spirit, I see the indifference that surrounds
death, and I feel indignant. But why?
Death, like life, only has meaning
with those we really know.

I'm afraid to die. I'm afraid to face my Maker.
I keep asking God for another chance.
But I know it's too late.

Nobody will live forever. Death often comes when we least expect it.

Before we know it, we are dying!

The fear that surrounds the dying process often indicates we are not *dying right!*

• *Have we shared our love feelings with family and friends?*

• *Have we made amends to those we have wounded along the way?*

• *Have we completed the spiritual insights that will take us beyond the door of death?*

• *Have we told God we are sorry for those things we have knowingly left incomplete?*

I'm convinced before we can face death, we need to let go of the religious abuse that has left us with an angry, punishing, and judgmental God.

If the door of death will take us face to face with our Maker, who wants to face a Darth Vader-type God?

"Tell me the God you believe in, and I'll tell you your feelings before Death."

PRAYER

You have accepted me in life.
I know You will accept me in death.
My fear of dying is not about You;
it speaks to a healthy fear of the unknown.
Some fears we all die with.

The minister whispered in my ear:
"Death is not personal.
It's part of the package we call life."

I'm not going to get out of this life alive!

• *Death brings an opportunity for closure.*

• *Death allows people to share feelings that can rarely be shared, or felt, in life.*

• *Death is essential to the continuation of the spiritual journey.*

• *Death is the final letting go of this life.*

• *Death is the final act of transformation that enables us to take all we have learned in this life into the next.*

Sometimes the obvious needs to be said: everyone will die. It's not the death that is personal; it's how we die.

A nun once shared with me the act of dying only defines the type of person we were in life.

• *An angry person will often die resentful.*

• *A selfish person will die with a demanding and obsessive attitude.*

• *A criminal might try to cheat death.*

• *A loving person will share a life of gratitude with those they have loved.*

• *A spiritual person will die with a knowing peace, eager to embrace the next adventure.*

We die as we have lived.

I'm a long way from death, yet I prepare for it.
In my meditation, before I sleep,
I forgive those who have caused me needless pain,
and I renew my connection to those I love.

329

How I die is as important as how I tried to live.
I want a good death. I want to let go with style.

Noel Coward declared, "I want to die in style." Wonderful.

Oscar Wilde affirmed, "Dying is the second most difficult thing I have ever done. The first was living." Bravo.

I want a good death.

I've said for many years I want to live a noble life. I'm not perfect, but I do have the capacity to do great and noble things. This is my goal.

I don't really expect to please all the people I meet on this earthly journey, but I want to live in integrity.

I know I carry a shadow, and I have my eccentricities. All this I can live with. But I do want to be the best I can be.

This is how I have tried to live. This is how I will try to die. The good death.

- *I wish to die with nobility.*
- *I wish to die in integrity.*
- *I wish to die the best death I can.*

I let go of mediocrity. I embrace greatness.
Even in death.

PRAYER

I know my death will reflect my life.
Hopefully I can take my life, my essential spirituality,
beyond the grave into the next life.
I've enjoyed being me.
I wish my "me-ness" to continue.

Racism

Chapter 9

I had to let go of all my parents had said about foreigners.
Only then could I see them as real people.

Whatever spirituality is about, it surely must be about inclusion. God created a world for us to live in together; division and racism speak to disease!

When I was a practicing alcoholic, I treated people disrespectfully. I didn't like who I was, so I transferred my shame onto others. I was a universal racist. *I didn't seem to like anybody!*

My family members, who are not alcoholic, were racist. They didn't like foreigners. As a suffering alcoholic, I absorbed their prejudices. When things are not going well in your life it is easy to blame others.

Thank God I got sober. The spiritual awakening that accompanied my recovery taught me to embrace reality rather than fantasy. This world is *created for people,* not just for *me,* or *my kind.* I needed to let go of negative and abusive baggage—which included my racism.

A Jewish woman who had been sober for many years had a great influence on my life because she shared about growing up in Nazi Germany and fleeing her homeland for freedom. However, her alcoholism kept her a slave. Only when she had faced her disease and surrendered into sobriety would she find freedom. Today she is able to forgive her persecutors. She understands their addiction to power.

Racism, like alcoholism, feeds on powerlessness and unmanageability. It always creates division and grows in insecurity. *Fear is afraid of difference.* Racism enhances the trappings of power; the boots, uniform, marching bands, flags and loud oratory — *and forever misses what is real.*

PRAYER

Father, today I own my prejudices and share my fears
because I desperately want to be real.
I know what it is to hide behind appearances.
I know what it is to be a hypocrite.
I'll willingly exchange what is nice for what is real.

*God's diversity is experienced in the various
races and cultures that populate the planet.*

I heard somebody say if you have a small God you will remain a small person. *People with a Big God can live in this world.*

It took me a long time to realize racists don't really live in the world, they live in a segregated mentality.

• *The white races are God's chosen children.*

• *We want all foreigners to leave so we can stay and prosper in our own land.*

• *Let them stay in their country, and marry their women. We will stay in our country and marry our women.*

• *The foreigners' food, color, speech, religion, and customs all speak to their inferiority. They are diseased and need to be kept separate.*

• *The Jew is a virus that needs to be segregated, isolated, and eventually destroyed.*

The spiritual person finds all the above sad, tragic, fear-based, *and small*. And it makes God small.

The diversity of this planet reflects the mystery and comprehensiveness of an Almighty God.

To travel and see the beauty of this planet, the variety of colors, plants, foods, animals, cultures and religions, is to experience what the poets call the *many in the one.*

And within this diversity is a golden thread that reveals the harmony of God's love for the world.

PRAYER

I cannot get enough of You in this world.
I thought I knew You when I lived in England,
but I discovered more in India.
Then Thailand. Then China. Then Morocco.
Always You are more.

I'm more than my race.

As a Christian priest, I feel so sad and ashamed when I hear some Christian people screaming racist slogans in the same sentence as Jesus. For me, Jesus not only breathed God's love, he embraced everyone.

• *As a Jew, he told his followers to embrace Israel and beyond.*

• *He proclaimed a Universal Kingdom.*

• *His spirit guided his followers to take love into all the world.*

• *He commended a foreign woman's love for her sick child as reflecting "the greatest faith."*

• *He condemned any religion that hid behind rules and refused to embrace new ideas.*

• *Jesus died promising the underdog, and the criminal, Paradise.*

Just when you think you understand Jesus, he surprises you with a new and different idea. He brings more than a religion, he brings a way of looking at the world!

This is my spirituality. Every day I'm discovering more and more about me.

I'm a mystery:

- *I catch myself saying things that surprise me.*

- *I experience feelings I thought belonged to women.*

- *I knelt in a foreign temple, hearing a language I could not comprehend, and felt at home.*

- *I catch myself experiencing the God I really believe in, in places other than the Bible.*

- *I know I'm more than my race.*

I gave myself permission to climb out of my little box that encompassed race, religion, culture, and family.

Only then could I breathe.

I love the foreigner. I am the foreigner. The foreigner is me.

PRAYER

God, you came to me as a foreigner.
You spoke to me in a foreign language.
You offered me foreign food.
You prayed a foreign prayer.
And I recognized You.

In order to embrace peace and serenity,
I must be willing to let go of racism.

Why did I ridicule people who looked different? Why did I despise foreign food? judge religions I did not understand? refuse to read their sacred writings?

Fear.

I had a fear that grew in insecurity. I felt safe knowing what my family had taught me, what my church had preached, what my neighbors had talked about, and what my language sounded like. Anything else was scary.

Then an Indian boy at school offered me some lunch. It was curry and naan. At first I said no, I didn't like foreign food. He smiled and asked how I knew I didn't like it if I'd never tried. I remember his smile. He had a gentle smile. I tried a little of his curry. I dipped the naan. Then I smiled. He liked my smile, too.

Racism could never quite compare to curry! I felt what was good. I intuitively knew who was kind. I recognized a smile that was real.

The Wisdom of Letting Go

How then could I deny what I knew?

From then on I started to let go of stuff that did not make sense. I could embrace religion without being stupid. It was okay for a spiritual person to think. God was far too big for my culture. Far too big for my religion. Far too big for my limited personal experience.

Amazing what can happen after curry and naan.

PRAYER

I recognized You in a smile.
It happened a long time ago.
But I catch glimpses of that same smile
as I travel Your planet.
I'm glad I keep discovering more of You.

*I should never base my self-esteem on making
other people look "less than."*

I suppose it's a quirky part of human nature that we all, at times, seek to look good at the expense of others.

How many of us have not laughed at somebody who got something wrong, while *we* knew the answer all along?

• *Somebody arrives casual for dinner and everybody else is dressed to the nines!*

• *We laugh sardonically at somebody's mispronunciation of a word or phrase.*

• *In a college debate, an excellent point is being made, the judging audience is persuaded by the logic, but the quotation used is incorrect. Forget the wonderful argument; we make the opponent look small for having gotten the quote wrong.*

I'm sure I've done all the above. And sadly, at times, I've used a racist slur or caricature to make a joke or feel superior. I'm not proud of that, but I know it has happened. How can I change? I was helped by knowing what it felt like to be on the other side of the fence — the one being exploited!

Recently I was with a group of friends who started to make fun of my English accent. Everyone was laughing at me. Then they made fun of my stature. I'm only five foot seven. They then connected my personality with "colonial attitudes." I felt awful. I wanted to run from the room. Tears were ever so close to the surface. Being made the object of ridicule is never fun.

Racism always seeks to dehumanize. It twists a small truth into an enormous lie. It always creates *shame* because it attacks who we are. Racism is evil.

PRAYER

I believe Your healing energy is in the world.
Work with the insecure so they might
discover their power and glory.
Let Your people discover they are angels in the dirt,
godlings ready to fly, reflectors of Your light.

When I walk in a city populated by various
cultures and traditions, I feel enriched.

I remember singing hymns in church that alluded to God's magnificent beauty and diverse radiance. The hymns affirmed the glory of diversity and richness of creation. Often the prayers emphasized the unity of humankind and a bestowed peace that brought nations together.

Healthy religion always speaks about a world becoming, a harmony men and women should strive to perfect.

Racism has always been the enemy of God because it wreaks havoc!

In 1999, a man killed a Filipino postman and injured many Jewish children with an automatic gun. They did not know him. He did not know them. He killed the postman for the insane reason that he was not white. He attempted to kill the children because they were Jewish. What made this even worse was the gunman quoted the Bible to justify his actions.

Contrast this story with an incident that happened to me in the same week. I was visiting a metaphysical

The Wisdom of Letting Go

church in Denver, and a young Chinese woman shared with me a book about the Buddha's teachings. She was a Christian, but she felt touched by a Buddhist story about forgiveness. Forgiving our enemies. Forgiving people who seek to hurt us. Sharing our spirituality with those who are in need of love.

The story is of a man who is about to be attacked by a gang from a neighboring village. They surround him and ask him what he intends to do. He replies:

"One: I can fight.

Two: I can run.

Three: I can love you.

I choose to love you!"

PRAYER

God of love, I reflect my love.
God of power, I reflect my power.
God of forgiveness, I reflect my forgiveness.
God of transformation, I reflect myself as
an instrument of transformation.

For years I believed I was not racist.
However, occasionally I meet my shadow side
and lurking among my fear and insecurity
is "the racist."

Recently I was driving in Los Angeles, and when a traffic light changed to red, I was forced to stop abruptly. Three Afro-American men were crossing the street and were shaken by my quick braking. They shouted at me outside the window. They banged on my car hood. They kicked my wheels.

Inside I became afraid. Angry. Shamed. *And I thought racist thoughts.* It all happened in a few minutes.

Where did those thoughts come from? Life. My life. Growing up in England I was surrounded by racism:

• *The blacks will take over if we let them.*

• *Why do they bring their superstitious religions with them?*

• *How can they expect to be taken seriously if they wear those funny hats and crazy robes.*

• *When we left their country it was in good working order. Now it is a mess.*

I had an English friend who refused to collect a morning paper from a local shop because the owners were Indian.

Some fish and chip shops in England brazenly advertise "British Fish & Chips" to distinguish themselves from foreigners.

I grew up with racism.

We carry our emotional baggage with us, and it is terrifyingly easy to walk from the *light* back into the *shadow.*

PRAYER

The "little racist" in me occasionally hurts,
and begs to feel secure.
In order for me to heal in Your light,
I must confront my shadow and embrace it.
In letting go, I acknowledge my racism.

Spirituality exists to teach the world to hold hands.

When I was giving lectures about religious addiction and religious abuse, I would receive letters that revealed the connection between fanatical religion and racism.

Indeed, it is my conviction that so much racism is bred and nurtured in unhealthy religion:

• *My husband would read from the Bible, and when it talked about the Jews shouting, "Crucify" at Jesus, he would become hysterical. "See," he would scream, "the Jews killed the Most Pure Christian. None of us is safe so long as Jews have power in this country." And our three children would be listening to their father!*

• *Don't ask me why, but my father and uncles would always lump blacks, perverted sex, homosexuals, Jews, and child-abusers together. If something on TV talked about a child abuse case, the racist rhetoric would follow. And all my family attended church on Sunday. My father's views were shared by many at the monthly Bible study. Interesting, my father sexually abused both me and my brother.*

Spirituality exists to teach the world to hold hands.

• *I've never met a spiritual person who is a racist.*

• *I've never met a spiritual person who does not respect the religion and culture of others.*

• *I've never worshipped in a church that affirms a spirituality that is not inclusive.*

• *Spirituality is the glue that holds this world together.*

PRAYER

God, I know You must be saddened at the hate
and division preached in Your name.
But You breathed Your spirit into creation.
We have the power to heal a divided and racist world.
Using Your sacred texts,
and the spiritual words of others,
we will return Your planet to You.

I've come to the conclusion a healthy religion
acknowledges the religions of others.
And seeks to learn from them.

My God is not a small God. And my Christianity can embrace the religions and philosophies of other cultures.

How?

It doesn't make sense to think otherwise. Jesus was a force for change. He looked to the future, and embraced a global thought. He did not think "small," and he did not expect his disciples to become narrow, rigid, or judgmental.

When Jesus said, "I am the way," I believe he was referring to what he professed, what he believed, and who he was *inside*. The "way" was not a six-foot Jew, with a beard, having brown hair! The "way" involved an acceptance of his teachings concerning love, forgiveness, who is my neighbor, where does God's Kingdom exist, perseverance, power to heal, *acceptance of foreigners*, and life beyond death.

This seems to be God's Truth. Jesus expounded on it in a unique way, with exceptional situations unfolding as he lived his historical life. However, we find similar sayings and happenings in Buddhism, Hinduism, Judaism, and Islam. What we have in common far exceeds that which divides us.

Rather than spending our time arguing about the differences, we should seek to build on a common spirituality that exists in all the great religions. The world needs to see a religion with a *loving face*, not a religion that condemns difference and diversity.

I've learned respect and tolerance from Buddhism, mystery and bliss from Hinduism, discipline and devotion from Islam, and forgiveness and scholarship from Judaism.

The "way" has many faces, and they all reflect love.

PRAYER

God, does religion have to be so complicated?
I enjoy the variety of fruits that grow on Your planet.
Must I determine one is superior to
or better than another?
Aren't religions similar?

Hate must first create disconnect.

Racism creates a division in the population when it seeks to justify venomous hate.

I do not believe it is our natural state as human beings to be angry, judgmental, or violent. However, if people are fed lies and hateful propaganda, over a period of time they come to believe it.

For example:

• *Jews seek to control the world by controlling international banking. They have never been productive in and of themselves. Rather, they make profit from the money the white races give them. If we do not patronize or support Jewish organizations, they will wither and die (Hitler speech 1938, Nuremberg).*

• *The black race is separate from the white race. Blacks are direct descendents of the sinner Ham in the Old Testament, and they are marked with the sign of Evil. White people should not feel pity or sorrow for the suffering of black people, because it is their destiny (K.K.K. Literature, 1984).*

In the above racist literature we see the purpose of this ridiculous propaganda is to create separation:

- *We are different.*
- *We have different feelings.*
- *We are pure; they are evil.*

Only when we let go of this emphasis on *difference* and begin to explore what the various races, cultures, and religions have in common will we create a peaceful and spiritual community. For too long there has been an extraordinary emphasis upon complexion, subtly connecting darkness with evil. Prejudicial remarks and violence have been justified by skin color.

Enough. It is time for the spiritual voices to be heard:

We are all created in the image of God. The wise learn and grow in the difference. Tolerance is freedom.

PRAYER

Reconciling Spirit, I bring before You in my mind
those who are filled with hate and prejudice.
I envision them surrounded by Your light of love.
Now I seek to give Your light words.

I'm proud of my English heritage.
But that does not make me a racist.

Sometimes I find myself becoming defensive concerning my English heritage. Especially when people are quick to point out the racism and exploitation that took place during our colonialization period.

Of course, I would never want to deny the horrors that took place within the English empire, nor would I want to go back to that period in English history. But when I say I am proud of my English heritage, I'm referring more to:

• *The legacy of English literature.*

• *The development of a justice system that has been practiced in law courts around the world.*

• *The spread of the English language, helping unite the world of commerce, education, and political stability.*

• *The individuality of the English character that is both amusing and reserved – quite unique in the European conglomerate.*

• *The sporting mentality of cricket that teaches fairness on and off the playing fields, and helped define "being a gentleman."*

Because I'm proud of my heritage I truly hope *you* know, honor, and are proud of yours. Self-esteem and self-worth are dependent upon being in touch with our *roots*, which must include our heritage.

PRAYER

You who have created the world, the different plants,
and the variety of creatures, have also created
humankind in marvelous variety.
May we always respect and learn from
each other's traditions.

I heard a man shout out that Jews are the anti-Christ.
Hate is often disguised as religion.

We must let go of the religious abuse that seeks to appear Christian and *pure* at the expense of others. Sexism, racism, homophobia, and bigotry often have their roots in a twisted religion that suggests if a person does not think, act, or speak in a predefined manner, based on a particular and narrow interpretation of scripture, *they are evil!*

I read a story about a young man who as a youth attended a church where it was taught Jews were not only the anti-Christ, but were collectively responsible for the death of Jesus. Over the years his hatred grew to include foreigners, Roman Catholics, other religions, homosexuals, and Afro-Americans. He was so filled with hate that he eventually became violent. He is now in jail for killing an old Jewish woman who was returning from her Synagogue in New York.

Hate is evil.

So much violence and hate is based upon twisted religion. What can we do?

• *It is important for all religious ministers and educators to preach and teach a religious tolerance based on respect.*

• *Whenever possible, the different religious organizations should come together to read, listen, and share their mutual insights into love, forgiveness, and acceptance.*

• *Websites need to be created that teach tolerance, and expose religious ignorance and intolerance.*

• *Spirituality often takes the guise of nicety. But there is an aspect of spirituality that demands being real. We must not be afraid to confront, march, speak out, and write articles that affirm inclusiveness.*

If it is true evil only requires good people to remain silent, then it behooves us to speak out.

PRAYER

I will not be silent when I'm faced with injustice.

I will not cower from violence.

Affirming my faith in You requires I walk my prayers.

*I need to move beyond what separates people
and embrace our commonality.*

It is never enough to pray about bringing people together; we need to *connect* our prayers with *action*.

For many years I've felt *spirituality* is the word that brings healing and wholeness to a community. However, to embrace spirituality, we must be willing to let go of artificial religious division.

Religions are often man-centered. Spirituality is the God-energy given to every creature. Religions often separate. Spirituality teaches the world to hold hands.

Racists are often people who are isolated. They don't really know very much about other cultures, religions, aspects of worship, interpretations of scripture, or spiritual paths to God. This isolation always leads to *dis-connection*.

If we are to heal the planet of racism and violence, then in the often ridiculed words of Rodney King, "We need to all get along!" And we will never get along if we do not understand each other. It used to be said a family that prays together will stay together. In a similar way, a community that is willing to pray, worship, and *discuss ideas* together is more likely to *connect*.

Words are often obstacles because they can mean different things to different people. If I say I'm *catholic*, many people will think I'm a Roman Catholic. However, the word *catholic* means universal. It is an inclusive word that holds the key to religious ecumenism.

Unity is not the same as *uniformity*. It is possible to have differing opinions and still hold together a *spiritual unity*. People differ politically, yet they are able to live alongside each other with respect.

Racism loves rhetoric. Racism fears dialogue!

PRAYER
You are the Word that became flesh.
Love in action. A love that created dialogue.
Today I embrace the action of Your life.

Racism is fear.

Racism is insecurity.

When I was drinking "alcoholically," I lived in fear and insecurity.

- *Why are people out to get me?*
- *I'm not as good as others.*
- *I mustn't let people know what is really happening in my life.*
- *My life is in free-fall. But I cannot ask for help.*
- *I know I'm not perfect. But others are even worse.*

All this *bottled* fear and insecurity eventually led to anger and violence. Rage was always lurking below the surface, and if things didn't go my way, then "the demon" was released. Always I found others to blame.

I think I understand the racist. *The addiction is power.* The racist feels powerless, his life is unmanageable. Feeling less than, he looks for others to blame:

- *Foreigners are taking his job.*
- *Jews accumulate wealth at the expense of others.*
- *Gays are spreading liberal ideas and disease.*
- *Blacks are demanding special privileges.*

The Wisdom of Letting Go

When the alcoholic goes to *his* support group and talks about his *disease*, he will probably be sharing the same things I've heard recovering racists talk about:

• *Always feeling on the outside of life, looking in.*

• *Dysfunctional family issues that created guilt and shame; the need to escape.*

• *A grandiose appearance that covers a basic insecurity.*

• *Developing a word-game-plan that blamed others for their misfortunes.*

• *A magical God who would save the day and make everything alright.*

To heal the racist, we must address his/her fear and insecurity.

PRAYER

God, You have given us the power to heal the
twisted feelings that feed the violence.
We seek to use Your energy in
connecting with the racist.
We speak as wounded healers.

The rainbow is the symbol of hope.

I suppose if I were thinking about the colors of racism, I would include black, gray, cold red, dull colors. Heavy with tears, blood, and sweat.

Symbols are important. We cannot live without the symbols of hope: a star, glittering cross, angel, sunrise, *and the rainbow.*

The rainbow has become the symbol of inclusivity, diversity, acceptance, and hope.

When I see the rainbow I think:

• *A world where all people can live in harmony.*

• *The acceptance of gay and lesbian people.*

• *A spirituality that looks beyond religion, beyond denomination.*

• *The face of God.*

We live in a world where hate has a variety of symbols. The flags of violence often burn brightly. We need an antidote.

The antidote is the rainbow.

Those of us who believe in a world where people can exist in harmony should consider proclaiming the rainbow.

- *On the rear window of our car.*
- *Outside the house on special occasions.*
- *A decorative pin on our coat.*
- *Symbolized presence in our act of worship.*

The rainbow needs to be seen. It represents not only what we believe, but who we are. Always the rainbow needs to be carried in our hearts.

PRAYER
God, You are alive in the rainbow.
Your energy is expressed through diversity.
Your world comprises THE MANY.

I had a mystical experience in a Hindu temple,
listening to worship I did not understand.
God is indeed a mystery.

I do not struggle in my understanding of a *Universal God*. I'm never agnostic about God's presence being the golden thread that unites all great religions. Never for one moment do I doubt God is being represented in art, music, poetry, and dance. *God is life!*

I do not need to understand all the aspects of God, or the hidden meanings at work in THIS PRESENCE; all I need do is be open to *the experience*.

Racism blocks this experience. It keeps people in the dark. It restricts the human spirit to the most basic instincts. Racism destroys the image of God!

I know this to be true in the same way I know lying is abusive, not only to the listener, but also to the *one who speaks*; that stealing robs everyone of *something*; that cowardice keeps a person from attaining dignity.

Racism, hate, and violence keep us separate not only from each other, but also *from God*.

Genesis reminds us what God created *was good*. Racism manipulates scripture to turn us away from the good, and choose evil.

How can we ever expect to discover God in a church, temple, or sacred text if we cannot see God in each other!

PRAYER

Holy One, I see You in all the colors of the rainbow.
Your energy is expressed in all cultures.
Your word is spoken in many sacred texts.
Yet, You are forever a mystery.

A friend told me God requires our participation in making this world good, safe, and peaceful. Also he shared evil does not exist without our full and enthusiastic participation.

Metaphorically speaking, the devil needs helpers!

• *Hitler was not alone in killing six million Jews.*

• *Many church-going people were active in the slave trade.*

• *The K.K.K. has survived because anonymous ordinary whites have continued to support it.*

• *Religious wars often terrorize those who are different.*

• *Racists are often enabled by friends and family.*

The evil of racism requires ordinary hands, feet, minds, and voices to complete its work. Racism is only a word until it finds a body to live in.

We all need to let go of our fear and confront racism.

When it appears in a joke, off-the-cuff remark, biblical interpretation, or casual conversation that presumes to include you, *it must be confronted.*

Confronted. Exposed. Destroyed.

PRAYER

You teach me spirituality is Your energy in action.
The healer seeks to touch.
Miracle is my hand grasping Yours.

We fear what we do not understand.
Racism will always follow in the
footsteps of the ignorant.

The key to healing racism is education.

When we begin to understand the scriptures are powerful words that move us beyond *mere literalism*, then we enter into the Mind of God in a most special way.

• *The wisdom we experience in the scriptures is also at work in other religious traditions.*

• *God created the world in variety and diversity. The richness of Spirit is discovered within the differing cultures.*

• *We are all foreigners in our journey to God. We are also, paradoxically, all God's children.*

• *Things are not wrong because I do not understand them. The mystery of God is often accompanied by confusion.*

Racism lives in the world of black and white. It is a small world, with a small god, for a fearful people.

Racism abhors mystery. It is certain. Never wrong. Always sure. *Racism plays God.*

The Wisdom of Letting Go

The more I seek to understand, the more I realize how much I do not know. The more I travel into other cultures, the more I feel I am known. With *the more* comes the mystery!

PRAYER

I know I do not know everything.

But some things I do know.

Racism is evil.

We are more than we appear.

I'm far more than I appear.If you meet me you might say I'm successful, handsome, charming, intriguing, and determined. But I'm more than I appear.

Racism. Would anybody think there is a racist hiding in me?

No? Yes?Yes.

I hate to admit there is a racist in me, but there is. If you push me, you will find I still carry the messages I received in childhood.

• *You are English. Remember that. People who are foreign are not to be trusted.*

• *Remember, Leo, that you are white. You will always be white. Marry somebody who is white.*

• *Europe is an ancient culture. Stay with your own kind.*

I never believed this. I was always attracted to people who were different from me. For most of my life I lived in the midst of racism, but I never felt racist!Recently, I've begun to speak out. I've always been attracted to people, colors, and cultures that are *different*. Why? Who knows. Who cares!

But racism seeks to stop this. It tries to make people *the same. Think the same. Feel the same. Act the same.* It does not make sense to me.

I'm afraid of racism because it denies the real me.

PRAYER

You are the God of more.
I feel You.
I am energized by You.
And today I know I must live You.

God is the many in the One.
Racial diversity reflects this truth.

I don't quite understand when people say *Jesus is the only way*. I know I'm Christian. I know I've read words that express this in the scriptures.

But truly, it does not make sense!

How can we become so *small* as to condemn all people who are not Christians to damnation, Hell, and eternal fire?

So, what do I say about myself? *I'm more.*

- *I'm a Christian priest, and more.*
- *I believe in Jesus, and more.*
- *I'm white, and more.* • *I'm a male, and more.*
- *I'm European, and more.*

One thing I truly know about me is I don't exactly fit. I've never really felt at home in any one paradigm.

And I don't believe I'm alone.

- *Yes, we've sat in a church, and heard the preacher. But deep down, we know there is more.*

- *Yes, we know we are white. But, we also know we are more.*

- *We are comfortable with our sexuality. We are happily married. Yet we felt connected with those who knew there was more.*

Tell me what I am, and I'll tell you there is more.

How much? Only time will tell.

PRAYER
You are one.
You are many.
You live in mystery.
And so do I.

Violence

Chapter 10

How can I let go of these feelings of violence?
They are who I am.

For some years I've been explaining how religious abuse tells you what you are not, and it is spirituality that tells you who you are!

We are not violent.

We are, I believe, human beings made in the image of God, the God of Love. Because I believe this, I also believe our essential nature is love.

We manifest love when we remember our roots, our divine roots.

• *The conflict comes when we grow up in a violent home, or amidst a violent community, and we imitate the negative.*

• *We see people fighting and we think this is how we should live.*

• *We see people fragmented and abused, and we copy that model.*

• *We see scant regard for the dignity of foreigners, little respect for their cultures, and we imitate this behavior.*

• *Strong is powerful, and we learn to despise the weak.*

Violence needs to be replaced with vulnerability and gentleness. It is the strong who forgive, the mature who can live with difference, and the healthy who seek to heal their violent feelings.

The message is: "We are not violent."

Those of us who believe this need to speak out more and proclaim the advantages of living in *peaceful community*. It is to everybody's advantage to live with dignity and respect.

My affirmations when I'm feeling violent are:

• *I am essentially a peaceful spirit.*

• *The violence I am feeling is the illusion of my insecurity.*

• *When I allow my anger to escalate into violence, I am disconnected from my true nature.*

• *I am not violent.*

PRAYER

I embrace Your call to peace.
I forgive the violent by sharing the power of change.
Spirituality requires action toward the violent.

I hate you.
I hate all you have said and done.
I hate who you are.

Sometimes I feel hateful. It's usually when I'm afraid or know I am wrong. I feel awkward. I feel defensive.

That *shadow side* of my nature that often defends and protects me can also be let loose to attack the innocent!

I remember meeting a patient in a clinic, and making an assumption that was untrue. I thought he was alcoholic and in denial. I didn't check his background. I hadn't really had much conversation with him before I made the assumption.

He protested. I argued all alcoholics in denial protest. I used his protest to confirm my suspicions. He got angry. I got angry. I was wrong!

He was not a drinker. The other staff members knew he was not alcoholic. I had not consulted them before making an incorrect assumption.

I was angry at his protestations. Eventually, fellow patients and staff members intervened and told me, "Fr. Leo, you are wrong."

I felt hate growing inside me:

- *I hated that the patient was right.*
- *I hated that I'd not checked before I had spoken.*
- *I hated my colleagues pointing out my mistake.*

My hate was aimed at everyone, because I was insecure. The professional "playing God."

Within the afternoon I had calmed down, and went to apologize to everyone involved. I needed to say I was sorry. Making amends is part of my spiritual life today.

However, hate exists in everyone. It's amazing what sparks the fire. We all need to be on our guard.

PRAYER
Eternal Healer, I bring You my hate.
I bring it so I can look at it.
In Your sacred space, I take responsibility.

Jews are the problem.
Let's just face this fact and get rid of them.

Stupidity, if repeated often enough, in the right atmosphere, being cheered on by a crowd, can appear brilliant!

Stupidity is the rambling thought of the non-thinking. Ignorant. Unintelligent. Insecure.

Hate carried into violence is nonsensical. Stupid.

Yet:

• *People are killed because they have a different color or religion.*

• *Women are regularly abused throughout the world by men because they are considered less than.*

• *Gays and lesbians are told God is Love; however, God does not love them, and what they feel is not love!*

• *Jews are still blamed for the death of Jesus. They are the scapegoat for unemployment, financial disasters, even Marxism!*

Whatever letting go is, it does not mean we allow these dangerous remarks to go unchallenged.

The Wisdom of Letting Go

Spiritual people heal dis-ease, and the above statements of violence are germs that will spread if not confronted. The healing is tough love.

PRAYER

I know Jesus was meek and mild.
But he was also confrontive and fearless
in his pursuit against hypocrisy.
God, Your spirituality is about being real.

You hate the fact that I am violent.
But you don't know me.
If you knew me,
you would understand why I'm violent.

Not knowing a person is no excuse for the violence. It is the violence that is the problem, not who you are!Don't misunderstand me. I agree a person's family life, religious abuse, and social upbringing all have a part in determining how we behave. However, we must never excuse the behavior because of the background!Letting go is never about *excuses*:

• *I rape and abuse women because my mother did not love me.*

• *I'm violent because my father and mother are alcoholic.*

• *When you're raised poor you try to get money any way you can.*

• *Don't blame me for what I've done. It was done to me. Nobody was there for me!*

Too bad! I'm sorry. But it is a continuing abuse to the community to excuse violence or hate by psychobabble.

• *We need to address the behavior.*

• *We should focus first on what is being said and done. Later, we can examine the heritage.*

• *Accepting excuses for non-acceptable behavior is an insult to the victim, and the perpetrator.*

• *Physician, heal thyself. Alcoholics need to stop drinking, then we'll discuss the other problems in their lives. Wife beaters, own the behavior, then we'll find therapy for their violence.*

PRAYER

You walk among us saying clearly:
"Stop, Look, Change."
I co-create in Your act of healing.
I am responsible for my healing.

Take your violence out the door. And go.

Just go.

I remember a single mother getting excellent therapy, and eventually discovering the healing power within herself to let go of the fear that stopped her from confronting her abusive teenager. Her message was clear:

Peter, I love you. I will always love you. But I have learned your drug use and drinking is not acceptable in this house. It is obviously not your home, because you do not treat it as a home. At best it is a motel; at other times, a wild playground.

Your abuse is making me sick, unhappy, and fearful. For these reasons, I am asking you to leave. I've arranged, if you want to go, a place in Safe House for troubled teenagers. I think you should go there. I cannot help you. I only enable you. I'm sorry it has come to this, but it has.

I will be involved in your treatment. I will attend group meetings at Safe House if you decide to go. I'm also getting help for my codependency.

I let you go in love.

When things are better you can return to your home. This is your home. But only you can decide to be a member of this family. Being a family member has responsibilities. I hope you learn what they are. This act of intervention is my responsibility to you. Peter, tonight at 5:00 p.m., a staff member will come to take you to Safe House. I hope you will be here to go with him.

PRAYER

I'm learning I am strong.
I'm learning I cannot please everyone.
It's okay to let go of people you love.

Love needs to be kept alive. Many people tell the story of a love that was real, passionate, caring, and gentle, but, over a period of time, diminished. How? Can love really die?

Well, yes. We need to nurture love just like we nurture our minds, bodies, and emotions. If we don't keep the connection alive, nourished, and sustained, it will atrophy. This is also true for friendship.

Love requires:

• *Communication and the true sharing of feelings.*

• *The interaction of positive and spiritual people to help support the relationship.*

• *Opportunities of space within the togetherness.*

• *Willingness to make amends when things are said or done that are hurtful.*

Hate grows in separation, insecurity, buried emotions, feeling taken for granted, and the awful silence.

This saying is helpful: "We always hurt the one we love." Sometimes we are so close, so sure of the love, so mindlessly ignorant in our sarcasm, that we don't realize the pain we are creating. Untreated pain leads to anger, then violence, then hate.

Let us always respect the feelings of love, offer prayers of gratitude, and never take the gift for granted.

PRAYER

Lord, I came so close to losing my beloved.
I allowed the hate to grow and I never shared my feelings.
My love was being suffocated. I felt afraid.
Then I heard Your voice.
Love heals all wounds.

When I hit you,
when I want to kill you,
it's because I once loved you.

Passion can be a killer. I remember hearing this tragic story:

A husband was insanely jealous of his wife. He hated anybody looking at her, speaking with her, or being her friend. He was always afraid she would leave him. Find somebody better. More interesting. Exciting. Better sex.

Naturally, she lived in fear. She hated looking attractive. She hated going out because she feared the attention she might get. Then she would have to come home and deal with his jealousy bouts.

Soon she withdrew. She never left the house. Never bought new clothes. She became fat. Sad. At thirty-two, she died.

Her husband cried at the funeral. "What will I ever do without her?" He had no idea his jealousy had killed her.

Oscar Wilde, in one of his more dramatic moments, said we all kill the one we love. Well, that's not true for everyone. However, some people manifest their worst fears.

The jealous husband did not just fear his wife leaving him, he feared her vitality, her radiance, and her style. *He feared her.*

Although he loved her, he feared her. And his fear eventually killed her.

PRAYER

Today, when I become jealous, I express it.
I know it's about me. My insecurity.
When I speak my fears,
they come into a healing perspective.
Thank You for communication.

I reached a point where I feared leaving the house.
The neighborhood is so violent.

Violence, addiction, and negativity are not only affecting individuals, they are also enmeshed in our society. Many neighborhoods are simply not safe. Nothing we can do about it?

I think there is something. Violence does not exist *outside* of human beings. Neighborhoods are not violent in themselves; it is the people who live in them. Churches, spiritual groups, people in recovery, parents, teachers, therapists, mental health organizations, and police all live and work in these neighborhoods. These peace groups need to *connect* and produce ongoing programs to address violence in the neighborhoods, plus form a *healing process* to help victims and predators into responsible living.

It's too big of a job!

Really? I don't think so. It takes a few telephone calls and an organizational framework to bring these groups together. Everybody wants the neighborhoods safe, except the criminals.

We have far more people demanding an end to violence than we have gangs. However, the gangs are organized and we are not!

If the spiritual life is about being positive and creative, then we need a call to action. I know from the many workshops I conduct across the country that people are *willing*. We only need to create the structure that brings us together.

Is it worth the effort? We all know it is. Let's begin.

PRAYER

You came so we could move forward.
You are present in our lives.
I am willing to activate Your energy for peace.

When I married him I knew he was violent.
And I hate the fact that I became like him!

There is a saying, "If you sleep with dogs, don't be surprised if you awake with fleas."

Violence creates violence if it is not treated and healed. There are some mental health workers, clergy, teachers, and social workers who are trained to counsel the violent. Most of us are not.

If we have a relationship with a violent person, it is so easy to *enable* the behavior or look away. Worse, we can become like them!

There are some things the untrained can do if they are living with a violent person:

• *Seek help through a professional organization.*

• *Attend support groups for those living with violence.*

• *Read books or listen to tapes that address codependent and enabling behavior.*

• *Plan an escape route so you can move out if the violence continues.*

• *Be willing to address your own violence with professional therapy.*

• *Protect the children.*

It is scary to contemplate the above because we are talking about letting go and change.

But realistically, what is the alternative?

PRAYER

God, I promised to be faithful until death separated us.
Violence is a form of death and it has separated us.
Now I walk with You to my new life.

I kill because I like it.

Hard to believe, but some people are bad news! Some people hate as easily as they put on their pants.

Of course, they were not born like this, but we did not know them before the violence! Violence always creates separation, fear, reciprocal anger, and death. It is almost impossible to live the spiritual life surrounded by violence. The answer: Walk. Move on. Get away. Find a safe place.

The person who wants to kill will eventually be killed. He or she will die on the streets or suffocate in a prison cell. Do we have a responsibility to the killer? Yes, and no.

Yes, we must try to do all we can to promote intervention, counseling, support groups, and ongoing therapy. It is in all of our interests to have safe neighborhoods. If we have the expertise to help in supporting the peace process, then we should lend a hand.

No, we are not responsible for another person's violence. And if we have our own problems and challenges— children, financial, educational, emotional—then it's okay for us to walk away. Get our own house in order. Become strong so we can help those toward whom we have a *direct* responsibility.

I am my brother's friend and lover; I'm not my brother's keeper!

PRAYER

God, I encountered evil today.
A human being so twisted and violent
I could only walk away.
Fear overwhelmed me.
Today I'm able to let others deal with
things beyond my experience.

It is not you. Not you particularly.
It's what you represent.
I hate rich people.

Some people are raised to hate ethnic groups. Their insecurity may even take them to that place where they distrust most organizations. Some Americans have been known to form paramilitary groups against the government.

All Jews, all blacks, all gays, all rich people — despised.

When hate comes at you in such a non-personal and illogical fashion, it is impossible to comprehend or understand. It is evil.

• *Regardless of age, profession, or background, "they" are to be destroyed. Exterminated. Never be seduced by their offer of friendship.*

• *All rich people have an attitude. They think anyone can be bought. They think they are better than anyone else. I hate them. When I see them I want to hurt them.*

• *All foreigners should be sent home. This land is for Americans. We do not have enough jobs for our own people. If they refuse to go home, send them to prison.*

Impersonal hate. Group hate. Illogical and indiscriminate, it spreads like a cancer if dressed in a military uniform, affirming a quasi-martyrdom for "the Nation."

Our best minds need to address this problem. It's been around far too long. The powerful use of spirituality, which has helped those suffering addiction and other forms of insecurity, needs to be employed in the healing of hate.

PRAYER

I let go of trying to understand hate,
where it comes from,
or why it manifests itself in every generation.
With You as my partner, I seek to heal it.

For two hundred years,
the white people have abused my race.
Now I'm fighting back.

When I encounter hate, there is usually some twisted logic that is apparent, some reason for the hate, some justification. But it's never the *whole* Truth. It's usually a piece of the Truth, a part of it. *And half the Truth is a lie!*

If evil as an energy exists, I'm convinced it operates in the above scenario. Evil, to do its job effectively, must appear logical, obvious, and rational. Evil manipulates Truth to be persuasive, *then follows the hate.*

Spiritual people are searchers of Truth. History is full of mistakes, prejudices, political lies, greed, religious abuse, violence, and hate. Every race and culture has reflected the above and been victimized by it. Some more than others. Some locally, others internationally. It is interesting to listen to scholars discuss which country was the most racist, which exploitation the most abusive, and which race suffered the most. Was slavery worse than the Jewish Holocaust? Is the Jewish Holocaust so different in kind from any previous or present tyranny that it must forever rank *unique*? Scholars continue the debate.

For most of us, hate is hate. People die. Children are exploited. Women systematically abused. The skeletons of the dead look very similar. Their haunting cries in history the same. *Hate is hate.*

Let's make our amends. Let's say we are sorry for our country's abuse. A race can and should speak for its culture. We ask forgiveness.

Then we need to let go and move on. Otherwise we remain victims of the violence!

PRAYER
I come to You with mixed feelings.
Proud of my country, and ashamed.
I feel connected but not responsible.
However, I know if I am to do Your work,
I must move on.

Why did you hurt me?
I was your child.
I loved you.

Probably of all the violence in the world, nothing horrifies like child abuse — the violence directed toward children.

Few children of alcoholics would disagree with above statement. Few children who have grown up in domestic violence would disagree with the above. And the wounds of sexual abuse *sometimes* last forever.

How can somebody hurt children? There is no single answer.

• *Some child abusers were themselves victims. They continue to do what was done to them.*

• *Alcoholics and drug addicts are rarely aware of what their abuse is doing to the family, let alone the children.*

• *Some adults get a high from hurting children. They prefer children to adults.*

Violence takes no prisoners. Everyone who lives with it has a part of themselves wounded. It affects children in the following ways:

• *They don't talk.*

The Wisdom of Letting Go

- *They don't trust.*
- *They don't feel.*

The healing agent for children must be spirituality. The abuse was never about them.

As painful as it was, they were the victims. They didn't deserve it. They didn't want it. It is a wound that came with their life.

The children of abuse need love. They need to hear bad things happen to good people, that wounds will heal in time. They need to be surrounded by unconditional love.

For them to let go, they need to see a happy, joyous, and free horizon— *that they deserve.*

PRAYER

My childhood wounds I bring to You.
I lay them at Your feet.
I let Your presence surround them.
Then I pick them up and carry them into my healing.

God is love.
But God is also judgment.
Violence is an instrument of God.

As I've said in this book many times, the Bible has within it prose, poetry, metaphor, and myth. Always its themes are accompanied by colorful language.

• *We read about God's anger and jealousy.*

• *We hear God allows children to suffer alongside their parents.*

• *Cities that house the good and the sinful are destroyed because God is angry.*

• *The good are tested with horrible torments.*

In the Bible we read more about God being a judge than a lover. That is the way the writers saw what was happening in the world. Remember, the Bible, although inspired, has a *limited* viewpoint; it was pre-science.

Many use some of the stories in the Bible to justify their violence toward others. They will root around in the Bible text to find a story or saying that seems to give permission for their hatred and abuse of gays, women, foreigners, Jews, even the rich!

The Wisdom of Letting Go

Let's face it, no book in history has inspired more people than the Bible, yet it has also been responsible for more deaths than any book in history!

Read the Bible with advisement. Always have one or two commentaries to help you interpret the violent texts. Seek to find God's presence in the writings of others. Experience Spirit in the world's diversity.

PRAYER

I read the Bible today.
I determined to hear Your voice in the readings,
and it wasn't easy.
Then a bird sang outside my window,
and I felt your presence.

I hate gay people. But so does God!
When I hurt you I'm doing it in God's name.

God is not about hate. Often we project onto God our fears, insecurities, confusion, and anger. People are good and bad. I've met all types of people in every walk of life, from every country and many cultures. Most have been wonderful; a few, abusive.

I was driven to the airport by an Afro-American woman who was talking about race problems in Denver. I was listening to her and I said:

"You know, the people who've hurt me the most in life have been white. Don't misunderstand me, I've had some problems at times with a variety of cultures, but the people who have caused me the most pain, the deepest hurt, have been white; often my friends!"

She must have thought about it, as the following week when she again met me at the airport, the first words out of her mouth were, "Fr. Leo, I agree! The people who have caused me the most distress, really hurt me, have been black. And yes, mostly family and friends."

I can acknowledge this today. But some people manipulate the hurt they have experienced and blame *the foreigner, the gay,* or *the Jew.*

The key to healing the racist is to get them to talk about their pain, their hurt feelings in childhood. Let's discover where the *twist* happened. I would bet money that in most cases it happened within the family or among friends!

PRAYER

God, I know You are love.
I know the hate in the world causes You pain.
But today I appreciate Your detachment.
Your children need to grow up
and tend to their responsibilities.
And we can do it.

There is no excuse for violence. What right does any person have to use force to get a person to do what they want, speak in a certain way, or believe a fundamentalist ideal? Violence is non-acceptable behavior.

It reminds me of the saying: "He who can, does. He who cannot, shouts!"

The person who uses violence is the one in need of help.

Recently in the United States we have witnessed violence in our schools: children perpetrating violence upon children. Where did they get this idea of violence?

- *Some suggest the violence depicted in movies and TV.*
- *Others blame the breakdown of the family.*
- *Not a few talk about single-parent homes.*
- *We sometimes hear about latchkey children.*
- *Others talk about the absence of religion and prayer in our families and schools.*

I believe the truth lies in all the above. I also think violence manifests when we have a *breakdown of community*.

People feel *disconnected*. They have gadgets that talk and make music, but nobody is actually talking *with* and *to* them. Neighborhoods exist without *real* neighbors! We are a society that has everything but is still *lonely*.

We all, including myself, need to find new ways to talk about God and make spirituality relevant in our world. *We desperately need the poets.*

PRAYER

I've always found You so exciting.
The challenge for me is to express that
excitement in my life.
I am Your message!
Only when the world has a connection to You
will there be lasting peace.

God is love.
There is no excuse for violence
in God's name.

Sometimes I want to get inside the phrase, "God is Love," and really explore what it means:

• *I know it's about being proactive in the face of injustice.*

• *I know it's about being real rather than offering a slippery nicety.*

• *I know it's about confronting racism and violence whenever they raise their ugly heads.*

• *I know it's about giving respect and dignity to religions and cultures different from my own.*

• *I know it's about speaking Truth as I see it, and becoming the love I talk about.*

God's love involves me.

What I must never do is fear the love of God. I know it is about pushing myself to the next level of consciousness, and not settling for what I have now.

The destructive energy of violence can never overcome the power of God's love.

I need to remember this.

PRAYER

I embrace Your love in the healing action
I manifest in the world.
My fears become apparent
when I forget who I am.

Asian people make me sick.
I saw what they did in Vietnam.
Today I see them and I just want to hurt them.

We fear what we do not understand. This fear can easily develop into a defensive posture that leads to violence. Jesus said to his listeners, "Having eyes, do you not see?"

When we look at the world with the eyes of spirituality, we see beauty manifest in the variety of life and cultures that make up this planet.

• *Vietnam experienced a war, but the war is not Vietnam.*

• *Vietnamese did battle for what they believed in, both North and South. But the fighting is not who they are.*

• *Asia is diversity. It reflects every aspect of human glory and greatness, alongside fearful defensiveness. Asia is life.*

Whenever we confront racism in life, we see a people who have chosen, through ignorance, to remain *small*. People fear what they do not know or understand. That is what keeps them small.

The answer to racism is *connection*. Once people begin to talk about their dreams for their children, their hopes for their country, the foods they enjoy and their methods of cooking, the music that inspires them, and *what makes them afraid*, we will realize how similar we are *inside*. Let's build the bridges that will end the violence!

PRAYER

I met a man the other day who spoke to my heart.
He shared my tears and reflected my fears.
And he was a Samaritan!

Violence is life.

No, violence is death. If we continue to hurt and maim people because they are different, ridicule and abuse women because they *appear* weaker, disassociate from foreigners because they bring a different religion and culture, *then we are lost.*

Jesus said, "I came that you might have life and have it abundantly."

• *Do we really think he was talking to only white Christians?*

• *Do we really think the love Jesus expressed was only for the few?*

• *Do we really think there is only one path to the God who created this amazing planet?*

• *Do we really think violence, in any shape or form, is compatible with a teacher who asked his followers to turn the other cheek?*

Everybody knows violence is part of the world's fabric, but I believe things are getting better, more loving, and more peaceful.

• *Women have rights today that were absent a hundred years ago.*

• *Gays and lesbians are more accepted, and are able to play a more open role in society.*

• *Racial harmony is growing and past injustices are chronicled.*

• *Anti-Semitism is on the decrease, and the vast majority of people abhor Hitler's Germany.*

Things are getting better.

PRAYER

God, when I think about the violence
that is apparent in this world,
I forget Your Spirit is pushing us
to a healthier place.
And we are cooperating.

God is love. We will only be happy when we love.

I heard a friend say violence is a *soul-disease*. Something went wrong in the wiring. Perhaps in childhood, adolescent rejection, failure of goals, personal challenges, or whatever — *something went wrong with the wiring.*

So many people, in contrast to the people who are violent, affirm God is love. What does it mean to say God is love?

• It means every day we wake up believing we are loved, and nothing can separate us from God's unconditional acceptance. Of course, implied in the statement, "God is love," is the desire for us to reflect peace and harmony in the world. And when we get off track, we make amends.

• We view the world as a family of nations, where we seek to learn and grow with each other. The harmony and serenity we feel when we view the foreigner as our "neighbor" diminishes potential conflicts. Of course we will have differing views, but so what? No one person or nation has all the answers.

• We know our belief about God, and the nature of a global family, assures peace and stability, not only in our neighborhoods, but

The Wisdom of Letting Go

throughout the world. There may always be minor conflicts, occasional revolutions, and small wars throughout the world; however, the concentrated energy of goodwill always creates stability and harmony.

So we have a choice. We can choose the path of violence, which always emphasizes the diminishment of some people, with conflicts and neighborhood hatreds, or we can follow the path of love.

Love God and your neighbor as yourself. This is the path of the soul.

We must make a choice.

PRAYER

Today I know I am on Your side.
I walk with my hand in Yours and
I co-create peace and harmony.
My cup is overflowing with this choice.

About the Author

Dynamic, challenging, insightful, and witty, Father Leo Booth is a priest cut from a very different cloth. He claims you don't have to be religious to be spiritual. He's as likely to quote from the Beatles, *The Velveteen Rabbit,* or Oscar Wilde, as he is from the Bible. His passion is to help us discover God and spirituality are not "out there" somewhere, but are found within ourselves and our world.

Father Leo is an internationally acclaimed author, lecturer, and trainer on all aspects of spirituality, as well as recovery from depression, addictions, compulsive behaviors, and low self-esteem. He holds a Masters degree in Theology from King's College, London, England, and is a Certified Addictions Counselor and Certified Eating Disorders Counselor. He is a national consultant to hospitals and psychiatric centers. In addition to specific inservices and lectures on religious addiction and abuse, Father Leo presents workshops, lectures, and training on a broad spectrum of issues to a variety of organizations and institutions. He is a contributing columnist to several publications. Father Leo has appeared on such television programs as *The Oprah Winfrey Show, Geraldo, Sally Jesse Raphael,* and others.

Born in England, Father Leo was raised in a home divided by religious arguments. Driven and ambitious, he became one of the youngest rectors in England. He also became an alcoholic and religious addict. After a drunken car crash in 1977 led to his treatment for alcoholism, he subsequently devoted his work to helping addicts and others who suffer from low self-esteem. From his work as both a priest and an addictions counselor, he has developed a new spiritual model based on Choice, Action, Responsibility, and Empowerment.

BOOKS BY FATHER LEO

When God Becomes A Drug

A challenging, insightful look at the symptoms and sources of religious addiction and abuse. This book offers tools for recovery from religious abuse, as well as a step-by-step guide to intervention.

(SCP Limited $15.00)

The God Game: It's Your Move

Father Leo's most daring book answers the oft-asked question, "Why can't I get spiritual?" *The God Game* explores moving from spiritual pawn to powerful player with God in the adventure of life.

(SCP Limited $15.00)

Spirituality and Recovery

One of the most popular of Father Leo's works, this book is a guide to creating healthy spirituality in recovery.

(SCP Limited $10.00)

The Angel and The Frog

In this charming spiritual fable, Cedric the frog and the residents of Olde Stable Farm meet an angel named Christine and discover the Spiritual Process.

(SCP Limited $12.95)

Treasures: Awakening Our Spiritual Gifts

Spirit can be found in the ordinary happenings of life: lines at the airport and Rudolph the Red-Nosed Reindeer. Father Leo takes you on an extraordinary journey to find Spirit in ordinary events.

(SCP Limited $15.00)

Say Yes to Life Daily Meditations

These 365 daily mediations on issues relating to alcoholism, chemical dependency, eating disorders and codependency provide the best of Father Leo: they are thoughtful, challenging, humorous, offering hope for
recovery.

(SCP Limited $10.00)

Say Yes to Life: Continuing the Journey

A ten week workbook for developing spirituality, recovery, and healing.

(SCP Limited $35.00)

Meditations for Compulsive People

A collection of meditations in verse with worksheets and process questions.

(SCP Limited $10.00)

AUDIOS BY FATHER LEO

Individual Audio Tapes $8.00 each

A1 Say Yes To Life
A2 The Twelve Step Lifestyle
A3 Spirituality & Adult Child Recovery
A4 My Life Story
A5 Surrender Brings Sanity
A6 Intervention: Creating an Opportunity to Live
B1 Recovery From an Eating Disorder
B2 Addiction: Effect Upon the Family
B3 Overcoming Guilt and Shame
B4 Relapse: A Spiritual Breakdown
B5 Positive Attitudes in Recovery
B6 Sexuality and Recovery
C1 Meditations for Compulsive People
C2 Say Yes to Relationships
C3 Overcoming Depression
C4 Overcoming Religious Abuse
C5 Creating Healthy Relationships
C6 Overcoming Resentments
C7 Codependency: Learning to Love
C8 Recovery From the Lie: Cocaine
D1 Creating Healthy Relationships: Know Your
    Boundaries
D2 It's Not What You're Eating…
D3 When Money Doesn't Fix It
D4 Self-Esteem: How to Achieve It
D5 Learning to Overcome Stress

Say Yes To Life (A1,B4,B5,C6)

Overcoming Religious Addiction/Abuse (B1,B3,B6,C4)

Using the Celestine Principles (D6,E1,E2,E3)

Creating Healthy Relationships (A3,A5,B2,C5)

Masterminding for the New Millenium

Awakening Our Spirituality

Turning Obstacles Into Opportunities

Insight, Wisdom & Harmony
(Based on *The Angel & The Frog*)

*Or create your own album by choosing any
four individual audio tapes.
Receive all four at the special album price,
along with an attractive case.*

VIDEOS BY FATHER LEO
VHS 55 Mins $39.95 each

V1 Say Yes To Life
V2 Meditations for Compulsive People
V3 Spirituality and Adult Child Recovery
V4 Creating Healthy Relationships
V5 Recovery From an Eating Disorder
V6 Intervention. Creating an Opportunity to Live
V7 Overcoming Religious Addiction and Religious Abuse
V8 An Evening With Father Leo

Annual Spiritual Empowerment Conference Cruises & Retreats

Each year, Father Leo presents spiritual empowerment conference cruises and retreats. During these
fun filled days, you will explore all aspects of healthy
spirituality, from the morning "Attitude of Gratitude"
to the evening entertainment. Each event's theme
focuses on some aspect of recovery from low self-
esteem and addictions. Early reservations are recom-
mended. Call Spiritual Concepts for current details.

Conferences - Workshops - Inservices - Consultancies

Father Leo works with a variety of groups and organizations, from treatment centers and therapists to the
general public, teaching how to create healthy spirituality. The Spiritual Concepts staff will help you with
any phase of the event, from choosing a topic to
suggesting marketing strategies, and creating ads and
flyers for your event. If you would like to share
Father Leo's wit, wisdom, and zest for life with your
program or organization, call Spiritual Concepts.

For more information, or to place an order, call:

Spiritual Concepts
(800) 284-2804

(8:00 AM - 4:00 PM Pacific time Monday-Friday)
2105 E 27th Street
Signal Hill, CA 90755
website: www.fatherleo.com
email: fatherleo@fatherleo.com